DATE DUE

DEC 1 6 2005		
	DISCARD	

DEMCO 38-296

CLEOPATRA

CLEOPATRA

Rose Blue and Corinne J. Naden

CHELSEA HOUSE PUBLISHERS
PHILADELPHIA

Frontispiece: Cleopatra has been portrayed by some as a living goddess. In this carving, she is depicted as the goddess Isis. She is a rare historic figure of mythic proportions.

Chelsea House Publishers
EDITOR IN CHIEF Sally Cheney
DIRECTOR OF PRODUCTION Kim Shinners
PRODUCTION MANAGER Pamela Loos
ART DIRECTOR Sara Davis
EDITOR Bill Conn
PRODUCTION EDITOR Diann Grasse
LAYOUT 21st Century Publishing and Communications, Inc.

The Chelsea House World Wide Web address is
http://www.chelseahouse.com

First Printing
1 3 5 7 9 8 6 4 2

Library of Congress Cataloging-in-Publication Data

Naden, Corinne J.
    Cleopatra / Corinne J. Naden and Rose Blue.
        p. cm — (Women of achievement)
    Includes bibliographical references and index.
    ISBN 0-7910-6320-8 (alk. paper)
    1. Cleopatra, Queen of Egypt, d. 30 B.C. 2. Egypt—History—
332 B.C.–640 A.D. 3. Queens—Egypt—Biography. I. Blue, Rose.
II. Title. III. Series.

DT92.7 .N33 2001
932'.021'092—dc21
    [B]   200147156

CONTENTS

WOMEN of ACHIEVEMENT

Jane Addams
SOCIAL WORKER

Madeleine Albright
STATESWOMAN

Marian Anderson
SINGER

Susan B. Anthony
WOMAN SUFFRAGIST

Joan of Arc
FRENCH SAINT AND HEROINE

Clara Barton
AMERICAN RED CROSS FOUNDER

Rachel Carson
BIOLOGIST AND AUTHOR

Cher
SINGER AND ACTRESS

Cleopatra
QUEEN OF EGYPT

Hillary Rodham Clinton
FIRST LADY AND ATTORNEY

Katie Couric
JOURNALIST

Diana, Princess of Wales
HUMANITARIAN

Emily Dickinson
POET

Elizabeth Dole
POLITICIAN

Amelia Earhart
AVIATOR

Gloria Estefan
SINGER

Jodie Foster
ACTRESS AND DIRECTOR

Ruth Bader Ginsburg
SUPREME COURT JUSTICE

Katherine Graham
PUBLISHER

Helen Hayes
ACTRESS

Mahalia Jackson
GOSPEL SINGER

Helen Keller
HUMANITARIAN

**Ann Landers/
Abigail Van Buren**
COLUMNISTS

Barbara McClintock
BIOLOGIST

Margaret Mead
ANTHROPOLOGIST

Julia Morgan
ARCHITECT

Toni Morrison
AUTHOR

Grandma Moses
PAINTER

Lucretia Mott
WOMAN SUFFRAGIST

Sandra Day O'Connor
SUPREME COURT JUSTICE

Rosie O'Donnell
ENTERTAINER AND COMEDIAN

Georgia O'Keeffe
PAINTER

Eleanor Roosevelt
DIPLOMAT AND HUMANITARIAN

Wilma Rudolph
CHAMPION ATHLETE

Diane Sawyer
JOURNALIST

Elizabeth Cady Stanton
WOMAN SUFFRAGIST

Martha Stewart
ENTREPRENEUR

Harriet Beecher Stowe
AUTHOR AND ABOLITIONIST

Barbra Streisand
ENTERTAINER

Amy Tan
AUTHOR

Elizabeth Taylor
ACTRESS AND ACTIVIST

Mother Teresa
HUMANITARIAN AND
RELIGIOUS LEADER

Barbara Walters
JOURNALIST

Edith Wharton
AUTHOR

Phillis Wheatley
POET

Oprah Winfrey
ENTERTAINER

"REMEMBER THE LADIES"

MATINA S. HORNER

"Remember the Ladies." That is what Abigail Adams wrote to her husband John, then a delegate to the Continental Congress, as the Founding Fathers met in Philadelphia to form a new nation in March of 1776. "Be more generous and favorable to them than your ancestors. Do not put such unlimited power in the hands of the Husbands. If particular care and attention is not paid to the Ladies," Abigail Adams warned, "we are determined to foment a Rebellion, and will not hold ourselves bound by any Laws in which we have no voice, or Representation."

The words of Abigail Adams, one of the earliest American advocates of women's rights, were prophetic. Because when we have not "remembered the ladies," they have, by their words and deeds, reminded us so forcefully of the omission that we cannot fail to remember them. For the history of American women is as interesting and varied as the history of our nation as a whole. American women have played an integral part in founding, settling, and building our country. Some we remember as remarkable women who—against great odds—achieved distinction in the public arena: Anne Hutchinson, who in the 17th century became a charismatic religious leader; Phillis Wheatley, an 18th-century black slave who became a poet; Susan B. Anthony, whose name is synonymous with the 19th-century women's rights movement, and who led the struggle to enfranchise women; and in the 20th century, Amelia Earhart, the first woman to cross the Atlantic Ocean by air.

These extraordinary women certainly merit our admiration, but other women, "common women," many of them all but forgotten, should also be recognized for their contributions to American thought and culture. Women have been community builders; they have founded schools and formed voluntary associations to help those in need; they have assumed the major responsibility for rearing children, passing on from one generation to the next the values that keep a culture alive. These and innumerable other contributions, once ignored, are now being recognized by scholars, students, and the public. It is exciting and gratifying that a part of our history that was hardly acknowledged a few generations ago is now being studied and brought to light.

In recent decades, the field of women's history has grown from obscurity to a politically controversial splinter movement to academic respectability, in many cases mainstreamed into such traditional disciplines as history, economics, and psychology. Scholars of women, both female and male, have organized research centers at such prestigious institutions as Wellesley College, Stanford University, and the University of California. Other notable centers for women's studies are the Center for the American Woman and Politics at the Eagleton Institute of Politics at Rutgers University; the Henry A. Murray Research Center for the Study of Lives, at Radcliffe College; and the Women's Research and Education Institute, the research arm of the Congressional Caucus on Women's Issues. Other scholars and public figures have established archives and libraries, such as the Schlesinger Library on the History of Women in America, at Radcliffe College, and the Sophia Smith Collection, at Smith College, to collect and preserve the written and tangible legacies of women.

From the initial donation of the Women's Rights Collection in 1943, the Schlesinger Library grew to encompass vast collections documenting the manifold accomplishments of American women. Simultaneously, the women's movement in general and the academic discipline of women's studies in particular also began with a narrow definition and gradually expanded their mandate. Early causes, such as woman suffrage and social reform, abolition, and organized labor were joined by newer concerns, such as the history of women in business and the professions and in politics and government; the study of the family; and social issues such as health policy and education.

Women, as historian Arthur M. Schlesinger, jr., once pointed out, "have constituted the most spectacular casualty of traditional history They have made up at least half the human race, but you could never tell that by looking at the books historians write." The new breed of historians is remedying that omission. They have written books about immigrant women and about working-class women who struggled for survival in cities and about black women who met the challenges of life in rural areas. They are telling the stories of women who, despite the barriers of tradition and economics, became lawyers and doctors and public figures.

The women's studies movement has also led scholars to question traditional interpretations of their respective disciplines. For example, the study of war has traditionally been an exercise in military and political analysis, an examination of strategies planned and executed by men. But scholars of women's history have pointed out that wars have also been periods of tremendous change and even opportunity for women, because the very absence of men on the home front enabled them to expand their educational, economic, and professional activities and to assume leadership in their homes.

The early scholars of women's history showed a unique brand of courage in choosing to investigate new subjects and take new approaches to old ones. Often, like their subjects, they endured criticism and even ostracism by their academic colleagues. But their efforts have unquestionably been worthwhile, because with the publication of each new study and book another piece of the historical patchwork is sewn into place, revealing an increasingly comprehensive picture of the role of women in our rich and varied history.

Such books on groups of women are essential, but books that focus on the lives of individuals are equally indispensable. Biographies can be inspirational, offering their readers the example of people with vision who have looked outside themselves for their goals and have often struggled against great obstacles to achieve them. Marian Anderson, for instance, had to overcome racial bigotry in order to perfect her art and perform as a concert singer. Isadora Duncan defied the rules of classical dance to find true artistic freedom. Jane Addams had to break down society's notions of the proper role for women in order to create new social situations, notably the settlement house. All of these women had to come to terms both with themselves and with the world in which they lived. Only then could they move ahead as pioneers in their chosen callings.

Biography can inspire not only by adulation but also by realism. It helps us to see not only the qualities in others that we hope to emulate, but also, perhaps, the weaknesses that made them "human." By helping us identify with the subject on a more personal level they help us feel that we, too, can achieve such goals. We read about Eleanor Roosevelt, for instance, who occupied a unique and seemingly enviable position as the wife of the president. Yet we can sympathize with her inner dilemma; an inherently shy woman, she had to force herself to live a most public life in order to use her position to benefit others. We may not be able to imagine ourselves having the immense poetic talent of Emily Dickinson, but from her story we can understand the challenges faced by a creative woman who was expected to fulfill many family responsibilities. And though few of us will ever reach the level of athletic accomplishment displayed by Wilma Rudolph or Babe Zaharias, we can still appreciate their spirit, their overwhelming will to excel.

A biography is a multifaceted lens. It is first of all a magnification, the intimate examination of one particular life. But at the same time, it is a wide-angle lens, informing us about the world in which the subject lived. We come away from reading about one life knowing more about the social, political, and economic fabric of the time. It is for this reason, perhaps, that the great New England essayist Ralph Waldo Emerson wrote in 1841, "There is properly no history: only biography." And it is also why biography, and particularly women's biography, will continue to fascinate writers and readers alike.

In the well-known tale of Cleopatra's first encounter with Julius Caesar, she is said to have rolled out of a blanket or rug. The dramatic entrance evidently made an impression that even the world conqueror could not ignore or resist. Caesar and Cleopatra would become one of the most famous couples in history.

1

CLEOPATRA LIVES

In the year 48 B.C., the great Roman general Julius Caesar traveled to the city of Alexandria in Egypt. He took up residence in the Egyptian palace and demanded to have the country's rulers, 21-year-old Cleopatra VII and her younger brother, Ptolemy XIII, brought before him. Cleopatra was hesitant. She and her brother were in the midst of a long and bitter battle for power over Egypt. She thought—with good reason—that her enemies would try to kill her if she were seen approaching the palace. Still, she knew it was important to answer his demand. Caesar was extremely powerful, and Cleopatra knew he could be helpful in her struggle against her brother.

According to legend, the clever young woman devised a plan to get herself safely to Caesar's palace. First, she enlisted her trusted friend, Apollodorus, to carry her by boat to the palace at dusk. Then she wrapped herself in a carpet and had Apollodorus tie up the ends. He then hoisted the entire "package" on his shoulder and marched unchallenged into the quarters of Julius Caesar. Who would think to question what appeared to be a simple workman transporting his goods?

No one knows what Caesar thought when the queen of Egypt tumbled out of the makeshift sack, but since he was a clever man himself and not above such trickery, he was most likely delighted by her wit and bravery. It is said that Caesar and Cleopatra embarked on a romantic relationship that very evening—a romance that is still known today as one of the world's greatest.

This story is just one of many that have survived in the centuries since Cleopatra lived. So much time has passed that the tales have taken on mythic proportions, and it is difficult to separate the facts of her life from the fiction that surrounds it. Cleopatra has been variously viewed as a goddess, a warrior, a scholar, a caring mother, a victim, and an immoral woman. Geoffrey Chaucer, the medieval author of *The Canterbury Tales*, believed Cleopatra was the model of a good wife. Centuries later, the famed Hollywood movie director Cecil B. DeMille, who released a movie on the Egyptian queen in 1934, called her the "wickedest woman in history."

In fact, Cleopatra has most often been pictured as a brazen temptress, a promiscuous woman who discarded paramours as if they were old shoes. The ancient Romans called her a prostitute, even a witch. Yet historical records tend to show otherwise. As far as we know, she had only two romantic relationships, one with Caesar and another with Marc Antony, a young Roman officer whom she married. Records also show that Cleopatra was a highly intelligent, well-educated, and capable administrator. She was also ambitious, strong-willed, and ruthless. Although she was not above using romance to gain what she wanted, it is clear that she was not simply playing the temptress for entertainment. Instead, she craved ultimate power—the power to restore to its former glory the royal line from which she descended.

Why do these different pictures of Cleopatra shift

from culture to culture? The answer lies in the changing values of the cultures themselves. For example, the ancient Romans intensely disliked Cleopatra because of her relationships with Julius Caesar and then Marc Antony. Many of them feared that she would so captivate these important men that Egypt would become more important to them than Rome itself. With Marc Antony they were correct to an extent—but it was perhaps Antony's own weakness

Though we will never know exactly what Cleopatra looked like, we have been left with many works of art depicting her. These are several marble portraits of the queen, which were exhibited at the British Museum in London in April 2001.

rather than any kind of "witchcraft" on Cleopatra's part that led to this end. Nevertheless, this outlook on Cleopatra persisted for as long as the Roman Empire held sway. Centuries later, during the 1980s, some African-American scholars speculated that Cleopatra, because she was a native of Egypt, was actually black. There may be some truth to the theory—after all, her paternal grandmother remains unknown. Most historians, however, now believe that her lineage was Macedonian and Greek.

The earliest factual portrait of Cleopatra comes to us from Plutarch, a Greek essayist and biographer (c.46–c.119 A.D.) whose *Parallel Lives* of ancient Greeks and Romans is considered a classic. Among the biographies in Plutarch's *Lives* is one of Marc Antony, written about 100 years after Cleopatra's death. The author regards her as a participant in a tragic love story and examines her words and actions. Plutarch's account inspired many other writers to examine the life of the Egyptian queen. In 1559, a French translation of Plutarch's *Lives* sparked a sort of "Cleopatra-mania" in France. Readers became obsessed with all things relating to the ancient queen. When Shakespeare fictionalized the tragic love story in his play *Antony and Cleopatra* (1607), he used as his source a famed 1579 translation of Plutarch's work by Sir Thomas North. As with other authors who employ Cleopatra as a fictional character, Shakespeare used the queen's behavior to reflect on the times in which he lived. His Cleopatra displays a wantonness that is viewed as an act of rebellion against the strict morals of early 17th-century England.

John Dryden, a rough contemporary of Shakespeare, also examined the life of Cleopatra in his most famous play, *All for Love, or the World Well Lost* (1678). His work describes the final days of Cleopatra and Antony, and it focuses on Cleopatra's battle for the heart and soul of Antony against his wife, Octavia, his friend

A carving of Ptolemy II and his wife/sister Arsinoe II. Judging from accounts of Arsinoe II's life, Cleopatra inherited her thirst for power and strong-willed nature.

Cleopatra on the Big Screen

Over 39 films have been made about Cleopatra, both in the United States and abroad. Some have been serious attempts to portray the historical character, but others—such as a 1975 flick called *Cleopatra Jones and the Casino of Gold*—have simply used her name to advance rather dubious plots.

The earliest movie to portray the Egyptian queen was the French film *Cleopatra* (released in the United States in 1899 as *Cleopatra's Tomb*). In the United States, the first film about Cleopatra was released in 1934 by Paramount Studios, and starred the popular French-born actress Claudette Colbert. The movie was campy, full of sin and romance, and wildly inaccurate in a historical sense. Directed by master showman Cecil B. DeMille, with the grandiose settings and lavish costuming for which he was famous, it includes some unintentionally amusing scenes. When Cleopatra meets Antony on a barge, for example, she presents a large tray of exotic foods, including clams hauled up from the sea in a net. The "clams" turn out to be dancing girls wrapped in seaweed. After eating and drinking, the stately queen develops hiccups, and Marc Antony (played by British actor Henry Wilcoxon) comes to her aid by slapping her on the back. The film was nominated for five Academy Awards and won one for cinematography. (Colbert received the Oscar for best actress that year, but she earned it for her performance in *It Happened One Night*.)

The most popular U.S. version of Cleopatra's life opened in 1963 and starred Elizabeth Taylor and her real-life romance, Richard Burton, who later became her husband. The studio dubbed *Cleopatra* the "most opulent, pictorially magnificent, and eye-filling screen spectacle ever made." It was also the longest, at four hours and six minutes—even longer than the epic films *Gone With the Wind* (1939) and *Ben-Hur* (1959), both of which ran well over three hours. Director Joseph L. Mankiewicz later admitted that he had hoped to make two separate pictures out of the footage; as it was, he cut the original six-hour film by two hours.

Most viewers had little trouble believing that as Cleopatra, the popular and beautiful Taylor could bring even the most powerful man to surrender. Perhaps the most astonishing scene is Cleopatra's entrance into Rome. Following dancing girls and warriors, she appears dressed in gold cloth and seated on a huge stone idol pulled along by hundreds of slaves. Although the movie concentrates on the queen's relationships with Caesar (played by Rex Harrison) and Marc Antony (played by Burton), it also presents some of the most spectacular land and sea battles ever filmed. Still, the long-awaited and pictorially magnificent film nearly broke the bank for 20th-Century Fox, the studio that produced it. Taylor alone received nearly $2 million for her performance. Although *Cleopatra* was critically panned, it was nominated for nine Academy Awards and earned four.

Dolabella, and his general, Ventidius. In 1899, the Irish dramatist and critic George Bernard Shaw also wrote a play about the queen titled *Caesar and Cleopatra*. It appeared as one of the plays in the collection known as *Three Plays for Puritans*, published the following year.

Hollywood's most lavish production of Cleopatra's story, Cleopatra, was filmed in 1963 and starred Dame Elizabeth Taylor. Though it was not a critical success, it seems the world and its imagination will never tire of Cleopatra's exciting life story: it contains all the romance, violence, royal opulence, and tragedy needed to produce a riveting film.

Plutarch made little mention of Cleopatra's appearance, and it is difficult to tell from the paintings and statues still in existence whether Cleopatra was the beauty that has been portrayed in films. No one really knows what she looked like, of course, although speculation has abounded over the centuries. Historian

Guy Weill Goudchaux, owner of a collection of ancient coins, points out that Cleopatra at least was not afraid to show her age: on one of the bronze coins in his collection, the Egyptian queen appears with facial wrinkles, even though she died at 39.

It may have been qualities other than physical beauty, however, that made Cleopatra such a lasting and captivating historical figure. Perhaps it was her bearing or her strong personality that led contemporaries to pass down her legend. She was apparently charming, brave, witty, and cultured. Plutarch said she had a voice "like an instrument of many strings," and that she had command of "a thousand" forms of flattery.

Why do we remain fascinated by a woman who lived so many centuries ago? By any standard, Cleopatra was unique. In a culture where women were commonly "seen but not heard," she was both highly visible and extremely influential. A member of royalty, she learned from her father how to govern, just as a son might have done—and she evidently inherited her cunning from her delighted father as well. Apparently the most intelligent member of the family during a time when girls were not expected to be smart or educated, she was the only person in the household who took the time to learn the Egyptian language, which was not the royal family's native tongue.

Cleopatra's personality probably has as much to do with her historical staying power as her royal background. Intelligent and quick-witted, she was also skilled in identifying and taking advantage of others' weaknesses. It appears that she was also an intensely driven and ambitious woman—although in the end her ambition would bring defeat and death.

In Cleopatra's brief life she was involved in war- and peace-making, royal intrigue, a ruthless struggle for power, violent and treacherous acts, and legendary love affairs. She ruled over—and then lost—an entire kingdom, and her name is forever linked with two of the most powerful men of the ancient world, Julius Caesar and Marc Antony. Although we know little of absolute fact about her, she lives on in our imaginations—on movie and television screens, in books and newspaper articles. Somehow Cleopatra's vivid, larger-than-life story reaches out from centuries ago and continues to enchant us today.

Two of the wonders of the ancient world are seen in this photograph. The Sphinx and the Cheops pyramid at Giza, Egypt. Hundreds of thousands of the pharaoh's slaves worked to construct the impressive monument and the majestic tomb. It is estimated that the Great Pyramid alone took approximately 20 years to construct.

2

CLEOPATRA'S WORLD

Cleopatra's full name was Cleopatra VII Thea Philopator. In Greek, Cleopatra means "glory of her race," and Philopator means "father-loving." She was born in 69 B.C., the third daughter of Ptolemy XII, king of Egypt. Ptolemy XII, who was known by the more familiar name of Auletes ("flute player"), was a descendant in a dynasty that had begun in 323 B.C., when Ptolemy I, a native of Macedonia and a subordinate of Alexander the Great, became one of three *Diadochi* (successors) to gain control over portions of Alexander's massive empire. Cleopatra would ultimately become the last of the Ptolemaic dynasty to rule Egypt.

Auletes had two wives, but it is not certain which of them was Cleopatra's mother. Most historians believe it was Cleopatra Tryphaena, who was also Auletes's sister. Although this sounds strange to us today, it was not unusual for royal leaders to marry their siblings. Cleopatra Tryphaena died shortly after her daughter was born; although Cleopatra had two younger brothers, born in 61 and 59 B.C., and a younger sister, Arsinoë, their mother is unknown. It was also traditional for members of the royal family to be given a common name—males in the family took the name Ptolemy when they ascended the throne, while most females were named Cleopatra.

The best way to understand Cleopatra VII and her role in history is to understand the world in which she lived. At the time, Egypt and Rome were the cultural and political centers of the world. For centuries Egypt was the most powerful and richest kingdom on earth. Its cities hugged the fertile banks of the Nile, the world's longest river at more than 4,100 miles. Each year during flood season, the mighty river overran its banks and left a layer of rich, black soil that allowed the Egyptians to raise bounteous crops for feeding themselves and maintaining livestock. Occasionally, however, the flooding was excessive or a drought prevented the flood season. During those years thousands of Egyptians would starve to death.

Although Egypt was ruled by mortal men, its ancient rulers, called "pharaohs," were viewed as living gods. (The word "pharaoh" comes from the Egyptian term meaning "great estate." It originally referred to the royal palace in which rulers lived, but soon came to designate the ruler himself.) During Egypt's greatest age, known as the Fourth Dynasty or the Old Kingdom (about 3200 to 2200 B.C.), workers and slaves of Egypt built many of the pyramids that we know today as marvels of architecture. The pyramids, testaments to the enormous power of the pharaohs, were built not to glorify Egypt itself but to protect the bodies of its deceased rulers. Ancient Egyptians believed that if a pharaoh's body decayed, then his spirit would wander alone for all eternity and would never enter the afterlife. To avoid such dire consequences, the body of a deceased pharaoh was preserved through

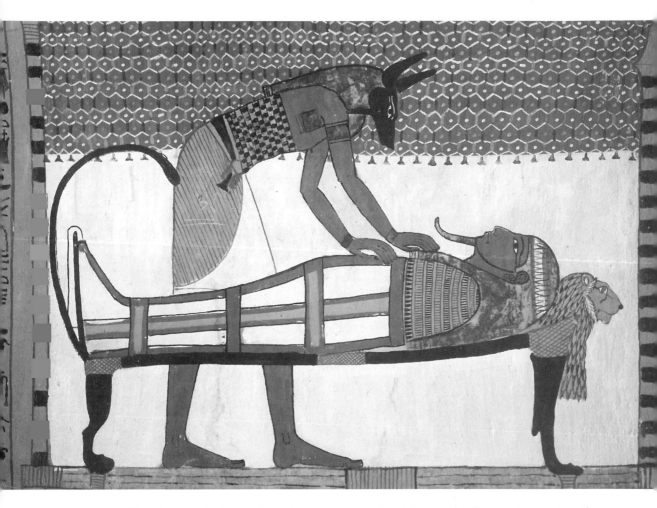

mummification and then placed in a pyramid with important objects from the ruler's life. Historians say that the Great Pyramid at Giza, which is actually the tomb of Khufu, the second king of the Fourth Dynasty, probably took more than 100,000 workers about 20 years to complete. An even older structure, the step pyramid at Saqqarah, was built during the Third Dynasty (about 2800 B.C.) and is probably the first important building erected in the region.

The era of the pharaohs ended in the third century B.C., when Egypt was invaded by Persians and

The illustration depicts the god Anubis leaning over a mummy. Mummification was the process of removing the body's internal organs, treating the body with a preservative known as resin, and finally wrapping the body in linen strips. The bodies were placed in tombs, which varied in extravagance depending on the person's wealth and socio-political standing.

the last pharaoh, Nectanebo II, fled the country. Persia absorbed Egypt into its own empire. Not long after, however, Alexander the Great—the son of Phillip II of Macedon (present-day Greece)—set out to conquer as much of the known world as possible. He defeated Persia and took Egypt as his own.

Alexander stayed in Egypt for only six months, but in that brief time he set the foundation for a firm and stable government, including naming Egyptian governors and establishing a system of tax collection. When he died in 323 at 33 years old, he had conquered most of the known world, from his homeland north of Greece, east to India, and south into Africa. He had also founded the great city of Alexandria on the Mediterranean Sea; it is here that he was buried.

Alexander had left no heir, and in 305 B.C. his vast empire was divided among three of his generals and their families. The Antigonids controlled Macedonia and most of Asia Minor, the Seleucids controlled Syria and lands farther east, and the Ptolemies took control of Egypt. These three kingdoms together made up the Hellenistic world. The predominant language of the region—and the predominant culture— was Greek.

Ptolemy I, one of Alexander's generals, became the first ruler in what would become the Ptolemaic or Macedonian dynasty. Of the three kingdoms, Egypt was by far the richest culturally and the strongest politically. Under the Ptolemies, it underwent an even greater transformation. The Ptolemies were active patrons of the Hellenistic culture. Perhaps the most important cultural gift they gave Egypt was Alexandria itself, the magnificent city where Cleopatra VII was born. The greatest and most influential city of its time, Alexandria had an enormous influence on Cleopatra's own life and her view of the world. When her ancestor Ptolemy I established a library and

museum in Alexandria, scholars came from all over the Mediterranean to study there. By Cleopatra's time the library contained more than 700,000 volumes.

Alexander the Great had chosen the site of the city that bore his name because of its deep-water harbor, its fertile land, and its strategic location at the edge of the Nile delta. By the time Cleopatra's father assumed the throne in 80 B.C., the splendid city had become a metropolis of more than a half-million people of

Alexander the Great officially conquered Egypt in 332 B.C. He would only stay there for 6 months before departing and dying at the age of 33. In the brief time he resided in Egypt, he set in place the foundations of an efficient government system.

many races and nationalities. It was a popular stop along caravan routes, with wide limestone streets and a bustling port. One of the biggest wonders of Alexandria was its famous lighthouse, commissioned by Ptolemy I and completed during the reign of his son, Ptolemy II Philadelphus (285–246 B.C.). Positioned on Pharos Island in the middle of the Alexandria harbor, the lighthouse was 423 feet high— the tallest manmade structure of its time and the first lighthouse in recorded history. Sailors could see its beacon (made by fire which was magnified by huge mirrors) from 35 miles at sea.

A causeway running from Pharos Island to the mainland divided Alexandria's harbor into two sections: the Great Harbor to the east, and the Safe Return Harbor to the west. Canals connected the harbor to the mighty Nile River. On the shore facing the Great Harbor was the royal palace, an enormous complex of buildings where Cleopatra was born and where she grew up.

From birth, Cleopatra was accustomed to luxury. She wore the finest clothing available, ate the choicest foods, and had access to nearly everything she desired, imported from all over the known world. The palace was huge, lavishly appointed, and extravagantly decorated. It included beautiful gardens, royal tombs, the museum and library, and numerous temples to Greek and Egyptian gods and goddesses. Alexandria was a gathering place for traders from many kingdoms and countries, and Cleopatra possessed an exceptional skill for learning many of the languages she heard spoken in the city's shops and bazaars.

The Ptolemies had little to do with their Egyptian subjects, however, except to exact agricultural output from them. Most Egyptians had little contact with the royal family and saw little difference between the way they lived before the Ptolemies and how they lived under their reign. Although Ptolemy

I, II, and III were strong and capable leaders who expanded the empire to Cyrenaica (present-day Libya), Palestine, the eastern coast of the Mediterranean, and parts of Asia Minor, the dynasty's power had begun to wane by the time Ptolemy IV assumed the throne.

The main reason for Egypt's political decline was the rise of the Roman Empire, whose forces had already conquered the Antigonids and captured part of the Seleucid kingdom. Ptolemy V, a poor military leader, lost most of Egypt's possessions in Asia Minor and along the Aegean Sea. After Ptolemy VI became king, a power struggle ensued in which his brother, Ptolemy VIII, seized the throne for a time. Cleopatra's father, Ptolemy XII (Auletes), ascended the throne in 80 B.C. after his father was murdered by the resentful Egyptians for having gained the throne with the help of Sulla, a Roman dictator. Thus a major goal of Ptolemy XII—and of Cleopatra after him—was to maintain independence from Roman authority by diplomatic means.

Auletes was a cultured and politically skilled man. He viewed politics as similar to the art of the theater, in that disguises and falsehood were part of an effective "performance." In many ways, however, he was also a weak man who gave in too often to extravagance and cruelty. Still, he held the throne of Egypt for nearly 30 tumultuous years. Cleopatra inherited many of her father's qualities as she grew up under his reign. Apparently Ptolemy XII's favorite child, she was by all accounts the most intelligent and most witty—and probably the most ambitious—of the royal children.

Cleopatra herself was, first and foremost, a Ptolemy. The very best of ancient Greek and Egyptian cultures lay at her feet. She received her education from the best scholars in Egypt. Servants fulfilled her smallest whim. She lacked for nothing, and there was little she could have wanted that would not have been granted her. But life during that period, as Ptolemy XII knew, was not perfect. Beneath the outward glamour and elegance, Egypt and the Ptolemy line were in grave danger. A self-indulgent king, Ptolemy XII watched as the Egyptians became increasingly restless and dissatisfied with his leadership. Moreover, the kingdom had been split when his brother became king of Cyprus, and when the Egyptians discovered that Ptolemy XI, his father, had left a will that ceded Egypt to Rome, Ptolemy XII found himself on unstable ground indeed.

Worse than the distrust of his people was the ever-growing political shadow of Rome. Ptolemy XII watched with mounting apprehension as Rome began taking more interest in Egypt's political and economic affairs. Perhaps the only reason that Rome hadn't taken advantage of Ptolemy XI's will and sent troops to take over Egypt was because it was struggling with its own political problems. For hundreds of years it had been a republic governed by an elected senate, which yearly appointed two consuls to administer the government. The consuls were vested with the power to name a temporary dictator in cases of political emergency. But the real power behind Rome rested with those who controlled its army, which governed the many territories it had conquered and occupied.

Rome's biggest problem during this period was widespread corruption among the men appointed to govern its richest territories. Experience had taught the Roman senate that these military governors were able to build up their own armies abroad and return to Rome, attempting to seize power. As a result, they reasoned, no one leader was honorable enough to be trusted with the vast riches of the Egyptian kingdom. Thus it seemed to be beneficial to Rome to allow Ptolemy XII to remain on the throne, despite the terms of his father's will.

In 60 B.C., when Cleopatra was nine years old, three Roman leaders decided to combine forces to restore order to the Roman Empire. One was a very wealthy politician and businessman named Marcus Crassus. The other two were military war heroes and generals, Gnaeus Pompey, and Julius Caesar. Together they were called the First Triumvirate, or rule of three.

Like his father and grandfather, Ptolemy XII decided that the best way to keep the throne and the Egyptian kingdom was to make a deal with Rome. In 59, he traveled to Rome to appeal to the triumvirate. Aware that both Caesar and Crassus were in favor of annexing Egypt, Ptolemy approached Pompey, who had defeated the Seleucids and annexed Syria a few years before.

Pompey was no stranger to Ptolemy—in order to stay on good terms with the Roman leader, Ptolemy had previously sent the general military supplies and funds. Now he asked Pompey to use his influence with Caesar and Crassus to keep Egypt free of Roman rule. He gave lavish gifts to the Roman senators and struck a deal with Caesar in which he would provide financing for a new military campaign in exchange for an independent Egypt. To complete the deal, Ptolemy XII had to borrow a huge sum from a Roman businessman named Rabirius Postumus—but he got his wish. Caesar persuaded the senate to pass the so-called Julian Law, which declared Ptolemy XII an "ally and friend of the Roman people" and made Egypt's independence secure, at least for a time.

Ptolemy XII's brother, however, was treated far differently by the Romans. They invaded his island kingdom of Cyprus, traditionally a part of the Ptolemaic dynasty, and transferred Cyprus's wealth into Rome's treasury—with no protest from Ptolemy. In disgrace, Ptolemy's brother committed suicide.

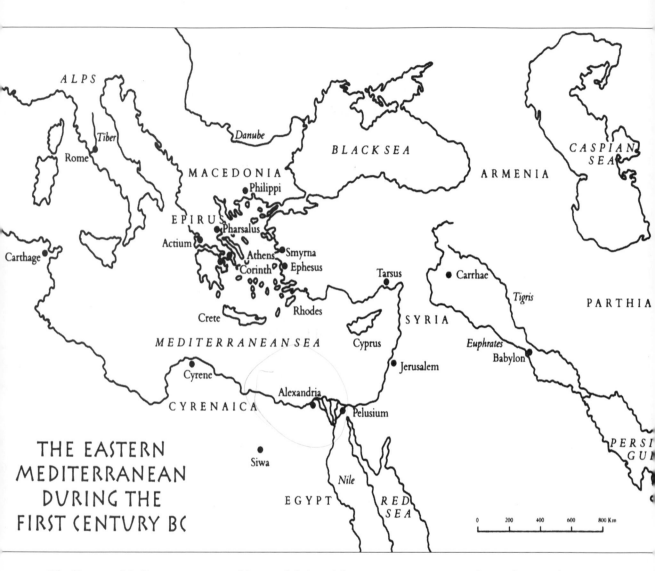

MACEDONIA

BLACK SEA

ALPS

Tiber

Rome

Danube

CASPIAN SEA

ARMENIA

Philippi

EPIRUS

Pharsalus

Actium

Carthage

Athens

Smyrna

Corinth

Ephesus

Tarsus

Carrhae

Tigris

PARTHIA

Crete

Rhodes

SYRIA

MEDITERRANEAN SEA

Cyprus

Euphrates

Babylon

Cyrene

Jerusalem

Alexandria

THE EASTERN
MEDITERRANEAN
DURING THE
FIRST CENTURY BC

CYRENAICA

Pelusium

PERSI
GUI

Siwa

Nile

RED
SEA

EGYPT

0   200   400   600   800 Km

*The Eastern Mediterranean
during the first century B.C.
The power of Rome had
become dominant throughout
the Mediterranean world.*

Alexandria's citizens were outraged to learn that Ptolemy had done nothing to help his brother. Even worse, they discovered, was that their king expected his subjects to pay back Postumus, from whom he had borrowed money. They revolted, and during the uprising Auletes fled Alexandria, leaving his two oldest daughters, Cleopatra VI Tryphaena and Berenice as co-regents. While he was gone, however, Cleopatra Tryphaena and Berenice proclaimed themselves

Egypt's rulers. When Cleopatra Tryphaena died shortly thereafter (some believe that she was murdered by her sister), Berenice assumed sole authority.

Historians disagree on whether the younger Cleopatra accompanied her father when he fled Alexandria. Had she stayed home without her father's protection, she might have had good reason to be frightened. It was not uncommon in the Ptolemaic dynasty for potential rulers to do away with possible rivals, even young ones. If Berenice had ordered the death of the older Cleopatra, why would she not do the same with the younger, especially if she were her father's favorite?

Ptolemy himself was now in dire trouble, not only at home but also in Rome. At first he traveled to Cyprus and appealed to Cato, the new Roman governor there, but he was treated with disdain. Cato told Ptolemy it was no use appealing to the Roman senate, for "all Egypt turned into gold would no longer satisfy the greed of the Roman politicians." He advised Ptolemy to return to Egypt and attempt to make peace with his subjects.

Ptolemy was stubborn, however, and he ignored the rude advice of Cato. He knew that he could not return safely to Egypt without support from the Roman military, so he traveled to Rome in an effort to make an appeal to Pompey and Caesar. Once again he was rebuffed: Pompey refused to help, and Caesar was away on a military campaign that would ultimately win Gaul (modern-day France) for the Roman Empire. Ptolemy's only recourse was to accept help from Postumus, the Roman business-man who had first loaned him money and who now feared that he would not recover the sum unless Ptolemy retained Egypt's throne. With Postumus's help, Ptolemy once again bribed senate members with lavish gifts, but to no avail. The senators turned to the Sibylline Books for guidance. Kept at the temple of the goddess Sybil, these prophetic books advised on important state matters. In this case, the books—probably reflecting the opinions of the Roman senators themselves—declared that "troubles and dangers" would come from aiding an Egyptian king.

Cleopatra's father next called on Aulus Gabinius, the Roman governor of Syria. Ptolemy pledged an enormous amount of gold in exchange for Gabinius's aid in restoring him to his throne. The gold persuaded an otherwise reluctant Gabinius, and before long a Roman legion was heading for Alexandria, headed by a 26-year-old officer named Marc Antony.

Antony was seeing the magnificent city of Alexandria for the first time. His visit may also have been the first time he met Cleopatra, then a teen, who would come to play an important role in his life. Some sources say, however, that the two never met during Antony's short stay in the capital city, and that their first meeting actually came later, when Antony returned under different circumstances. Finally, in 55 B.C., with the force of Rome now behind him, Ptolemy XII was again the king of Egypt. Among his first acts after being restored to the throne was to have his daughter, Berenice, executed.

Fourteen-year-old Cleopatra VII was now the eldest of Ptolemy's four surviving children. It is highly likely that she knew about the grim events that had transpired before her father regained his throne. She had watched him struggle over the years with unhappy and resentful subjects and with the burden of repaying a staggering amount of money to those from whom he had borrowed. She was well aware of the dangers and difficulties of ruling Egypt.

In 52 B.C. Ptolemy drew up a will in an effort to

prevent Rome from seizing Egypt after his death. The following year, he died. Cleopatra, now 18 years old, and her 10-year-old brother, Ptolemy, became queen and king of Egypt.

The Ptolemies had adopted some of the practices of the ancient pharaohs in an attempt to preserve absolute rule within the family and maintain political stability. One practice was that of the deification of leaders. As the pharaohs had done, the Ptolemies "bestowed" upon themselves a religious authority to rule Egypt in addition to their political control. When Cleopatra became queen, for example, she declared herself Isis, the Egyptian goddess of motherhood and fertility. With her brother, Osiris, Isis was ruler of earth and sky. The practice of marrying among siblings also originated with the pharaohs of ancient Egypt. When Cleopatra's father died and she and her brother inherited the kingdom, they were also married according to the ancient custom. Cleopatra became Cleopatra VII; her brother became Ptolemy XIII.

Cleopatra was in an uneasy position: she was not only very young, but she was also a woman, and there were many powerful men in the Egyptian court who craved the power she now held. Her brother was far too young to be an effective ally against these men— and before long, he would become her enemy. Because Ptolemy XIII was still a child, Egyptian law required that a regency council be appointed to help him rule. Three men made up the Council: Theodotus, the boy's Greek tutor; Achillas, commander of the Egyptian forces; and Pothinus, minister of finance and the kingdom's most powerful man. The three men wasted no time in manipulating the easily swayed boy and attempting to take control of Egypt. They could not, however, control the independent-minded Cleopatra.

An intelligent and strong-willed young woman,

Cleopatra's brother/husband Ptolemy XIII is carved into this wall at the Temple of Sobek and Horus, Kom Ombo. He is depicted as being "purified" by the two gods. At the time of his father Ptolemy XII's death, he was 10 years old. He was surrounded by self-seeking, ambitious male advisors who would soon manipulate the boy to go against his sister/wife Cleopatra.

Cleopatra would need to draw on all her courage and determination to battle the powerful men aligned against her. She was alone now, without her father or her childhood guardians to protect her. She wasted no time. When she took the throne, she made great efforts to endear herself to the Egyptian people, who had long since grown resentful of the Ptolemies who had never bothered to concern themselves with the lives of their subjects. Cleopatra honored Egyptian customs and showed reverence for the people's gods and goddesses. Yet at every turn, the powerful

Pothinus discredited her, blaming the new queen for every ill that befell the country.

Even the mighty Nile seemed against her. During her first two years as queen, the river did not flood enough to irrigate the fields, and the resulting crops were scarce. Egyptians began starving to death, agricultural workers were unable to pay their taxes, and many of them went into hiding for fear of retribution. The members of the regency council took advantage of the misfortunes of Egypt and publicly blamed Cleopatra in an effort to discredit her before her subjects.

Cleopatra soon suspected that the council was looking for a way to kill her. With no one to support her, she fled the country and escaped into the desert. Theodotus, Achillas, and Pothinus believed they were at last rid of the young queen and could now rule Egypt through the young Ptolemy XIII. But they had sorely underestimated Cleopatra.

The exiled queen first traveled to the Roman province of Syria, where she found backers to help her raise her own army in return for offering to share Egypt's wealth once she was restored to the throne. Cleopatra began to face the fact that Rome, not Egypt, was the central power of the Mediterranean world. Therefore, she reasoned, would it not make sense to ally herself with Rome rather than fight it?

Fortunately for Cleopatra, the tumultuous situation in Rome would work to her advantage. The empire was once again in turmoil, and Caesar and Pompey were engaged in a civil war against one another. They would both soon need to seek grain and other food from outside the empire to feed their troops. Sooner or later, one of them would seek help—and Cleopatra knew that both would surely be grateful to receive Egypt's cooperation.

By 48 B.C., Cleopatra had raised a substantial

Libraries of the Ancient World

Probably the greatest wonder of Egypt's capital was the library of Alexandria. During Cleopatra VII's lifetime, the library held more than 700,000 books in the form of scrolls of papyrus and vellum—about 10 times the number of books in all of Europe. The library was established by Ptolemy I and flourished under the reign of his son, Ptolemy II Philadelphus. The Ptolemies aimed to collect all of Greek literature in the best copies available and to arrange them systematically. Situated in a temple called the Mouseion, the library was staffed by Greek writers and scholars, including the most outstanding scholar of the time, Aristarchus of Samothrace (d.145 B.C.). Scholars from all over the known world came to the library of Alexandria to take advantage of the vast repository of information.

The magnificent library came to a sad end, however. No one is certain exactly what happened, but by the fourth century A.D., it had been badly damaged, either by earthquake or fire, and many of the books in the collection were destroyed. The Christian emperor Theodosius I believed that the library's annex contained pagan documents, and thus ordered 200,000 priceless scrolls to be burned. The rest of the books were destroyed by Arabs who conquered Egypt several hundred years later.

The only rival of the Alexandria library during Cleopatra's time was at Pergamum in Asia Minor. Established and expanded during the reigns of Attalus I (d. 197 B.C.) and Eumenes II (d. 159 B.C.), it was reportedly where parchment, a new type of writing material made from the processed skins of sheep or goats, was developed. Ptolemy Philadelphus had banned the export of papyrus, a sedge plant native to the Nile valley that was cut into strips and pressed into sheets or scrolls for writing. The ban helped to make parchment more popular, and it also proved to be more lasting than papyrus. Although the entire Pergamum library was granted to the Roman people in 133 B.C., Plutarch recorded that Marc Antony seized about 200,000 scrolls from its collection and donated them to the Alexandria library as a gift to Cleopatra.

Although Rome did not have any outstanding public libraries at the time, many wealthy and prominent Roman citizens found it fashionable to own private collections, and many of them opened their doors to those who wished to study in there. Julius Caesar died before his plans for a public library in Rome could be realized, but five years after his death Asinius Pollio managed to construct one. Later emperors also established libraries: for example, Trajan built one in 100 A.D. that lasted for at least 300 years.

army. Determined to regain the throne, she led the army to Pelusium in northern Egypt in preparation for fighting her brother and his regents for control of the kingdom. Cleopatra knew that the Ptolemy dynasty was not as powerful and influential as it had once been. The glorious days of Egypt's ascendancy were gone, and Rome was now the world's great power. But the queen held a burning desire to restore Egypt to its former splendor and influence. She was convinced that she would be the one ruler who could honor her ancestors by renewing the Ptolemaic reign, and she was determined to do so by whatever means were necessary. Cleopatra VII did not know, as she readied her forces for battle, that the two Romans with whom she would cast her lot during this struggle would change her life forever—and secure her place in world history.

In this original 17th-century painting by Cortona, two of the most powerful people of their time—Caesar and Cleopatra—join hands. With Caesar's aid, Cleopatra was able to ascend the Eygptian throne. Her brother/husband was killed in battle by Caesar's troops and her sister Arsinoe was exiled to Rome.

3

CAESAR AND CLEOPATRA

Mention Caesar and Cleopatra and most people call to mind one of the world's great legendary romances. There was much more, however, to the relationship between the 52-year-old leader of Rome and the 19-year-old queen of Egypt. In fact, romance may have been the least important aspect of their involvement.

Nearly everyone has heard of Julius Caesar. Most people know that he was a great Roman general. He was also a dictator who believed that any method, no matter how cruel, was justified to attain and keep power. For this reason, the name "Caesar" is often used today to refer to someone who is all-powerful, or who aspires to be so. Bullies, for example, are sometimes called "little Caesars." Yet, Julius Caesar was also a brilliant general and a capable and skilled statesman. Many dictators dream of ruling the world; Caesar effectively did just that, or at least he ruled the Mediterranean region, which was recognized as the only "civilized" world in his day. In doing so, Julius Caesar changed the course of European history and became a larger-than-life figure—one whom we would know more about than we would of Cleopatra.

Gaius Julius Caesar was born to a noble Roman family in 100 B.C., on the 12th of Quintilis (the Roman name for the period we call July). At his birth, the Roman Empire had already been established as one of the greatest powers in history. According to legend, the city of Rome was founded in 753 B.C. by twins named Romulus and Remus, who were reared by a she-wolf. Over centuries, Rome grew from a small town on the Tiber River in central Italy into an empire that at its height included England, much of continental Europe, most of northern Africa, and the islands of the Mediterranean Sea. The republic itself was established in 509 B.C. Rome became an empire in 27 B.C. It was a powerful political force for many centuries, until the fifth century A.D.

Caesar's family members were patricians, or landowners. This class of citizen formed the elite legislative body called the senate. The other ruling body, the popular assembly, was made up of common people (those who did not own land). Modern-day Great Britain, with its House of Lords and House of Commons, is loosely modeled on this Roman system. Together, the Roman senate and assembly voted on new laws and elected consuls, a highly sought-after position in the Roman government. Consuls served for two-year terms and had a broad range of power and control.

Julius Caesar was 15 when his father died, and he was forced to choose a career. Although his family had hoped he would become a priest, he chose politics instead. His uncle Marius was head of the political party that purported to represent the common people, and when Marius died a year after Julius's father, he left the leadership to Lucius Cornelius Cinna. Julius, at 16 years old, married Cinna's daughter, Cornelia, in part to gain access to political power. During a civil war, Cinna was executed by Lucius Cornelius Sulla, who ordered Julius to divorce his wife. The young man refused.

Caesar's refusal may have been out of love for his wife—but it may also have been a political move. Regardless of the reason, the young man's defiance of a powerful Roman leader forced him to flee Rome until conditions were safer. He joined the army and spent time studying on the island of Rhodes in the Aegean Sea. He would only return to Rome after he received word that Sulla had died. By this time it was 73 B.C., and Julius was a 26-year-old seasoned military veteran. In 67 B.C., after Cornelia died, Caesar remarried. His second wife, Pompeia, was the daughter of one of Rome's wealthiest families, and Julius worked hard to win favor with powerful men and earn the admiration and respect of the Roman people. In 59 B.C., he was rewarded for his efforts by being elected consul.

By this time, Caesar had divorced his second wife and married Calpurnia, the daughter of a former governor who supported the idea of a triumvirate, or three-man rule. Caesar agreed with the concept. Having worked to gain the friendship and trust of Rome's two most powerful men, Gnaeus Pompey and Marcus Crassus, Caesar was now positioned to join forces with them. The three created the First Triumvirate.

But Julius Caesar, now 42, was still not content. He believed that a true leader of Rome also had to be a successful military conqueror. In 58 B.C., he set his sights to the north of Rome to Gaul, launching a long and bitter campaign that ultimately added 200,000 square miles to Rome's territory and resulted in the deaths of about one million people. From Gaul, Caesar made raids into Britain as well. He was made governor of the Gallic provinces, and his reputation as a great military leader was now firmly established.

Despite his conquests, however, Caesar had been away from the seat of power in Rome for nearly a decade. Much had changed in his absence. Crassus had sought the same kind of military glory as Caesar had by invading the Parthian Empire (present-day Iran and Iraq), but he was soundly defeated and died in 53 B.C., along with 30,000 Roman soldiers. The loss was a disgrace for the Roman Empire, and with Crassus's death the First Triumvirate was dissolved. Caesar's friends in the senate passed a bill that allowed him to run for consulship even though he was absent from Rome, but the senate's conservative members, including Pompey, refused to honor it. Marc Antony argued on Caesar's behalf, but to no avail. As a result, Caesar and Pompey became fierce enemies. In 50 B.C., the Senate demanded that Caesar relinquish command of his army. He refused. The following year, Pompey became a virtual dictator in Rome, and Caesar prepared to invade the city.

Marc Antony and other allies of Caesar fled Rome and joined the general on the banks of the Rubicon River in north-central Italy, which was recognized as the dividing line between the Gallic provinces and Italy. Caesar knew that crossing the Rubicon would spark a civil war. In fact, such an act would be considered treason against the Roman government, which had a law prohibiting a governor of a province, as Caesar was in Gaul, from commanding troops outside his borders. "The die is cast," Caesar is said to have remarked as he led his army across the river. (Today, the phrase "crossing the Rubicon" means taking an irrevocable step.)

Unwilling to engage Caesar in battle until he had increased the strength of his own forces, Pompey retreated across the Adriatic Sea and turned to other governments for aid. Among them was Egypt, where

Cleopatra was still in power. When Pompey sent his son Gnaeus to the queen for help, she immediately dispatched 60 ships filled with grain and sent 500 men from Alexandria to aid Pompey. Caesar continued his pursuit, and ultimately the two men and their armies engaged in battle at Pharsalus in early 48 B.C. Pompey's army was routed, but he managed to escape to Cyprus. From there, he sailed for Egypt, where he hoped to be given refuge.

Cleopatra, meanwhile, was preparing to confront her brother's forces in battle at Pelusium, where she had assembled her own army. Just before the battle, Pompey's ship arrived off the Egyptian coast. He sent

A "family portrait" is carved on the wall of the Hathor Temple, Dendera (332-330 B.C.): in it one sees Ptolemy XVI, Caesarion (son of Caesar and Cleopatra). While the goddess Hathor looks on, another pharaoh offers incense to the gods.

a message to Ptolemy XIII and his regents asking for safe conduct to their camp. The request threw the regents into a quandary. If they provided asylum for Pompey, they risked incurring the wrath of the powerful Caesar. If they turned him away, however, they knew he would immediately seek Cleopatra's help. With the combined forces of Pompey and Cleopatra arrayed against them, the banished queen could well win the struggle for Egypt's throne.

After much discussion, the regents devised a plan. Achillas, one of the regents, took a small boat to Pompey's ship, where Pompey and his wife, Cornelia, awaited a reply. Achillas welcomed Pompey to Egypt and rowed him ashore. As soon as they reached land, Pompey was beheaded, as Cornelia screamed in horror from her vantage point on the ship.

Days later, Caesar arrived in Alexandria and sought Pompey at the royal palace. Instead, he was presented with Pompey's severed head and his signet ring. The regents had believed that the "gift" of Pompey's death would not only rid them of the threat of Pompey aligning himself with Cleopatra, but it would also appease Caesar and keep him from meddling in Egypt's affairs.

They were wrong. Caesar was glad that Pompey was no longer a threat, but the idea that the noble Roman had been slain at the hands of Egyptians, whom he considered inferior people, enraged the general. Caesar brought a small force into Alexandria and established himself in the palace. He declared that Egypt had never fully repaid the money that Ptolemy XII had promised them, and he was determined to stay in Alexandria until he received it. The Egyptians, meanwhile, viewed the procession of Romans as an insult to their king. Infuriated by the affront, they rioted, killing a number of Roman soldiers.

Caesar decided it was wise to wait until the riots

subsided. In the meantime, since he was the leading representative of Rome in Egypt, he announced that he would settle the conflict between Cleopatra and her brother. He ordered the royal siblings to be brought before him. Cleopatra knew very well that her life would be in grave danger if she attempted to reach the palace on her own, so she devised the plan by which she would be stowed in a rolled-up carpet and carried before Caesar.

The powerful general and the young queen were immediately attracted to each other. In addition to the physical attraction, Caesar saw in Cleopatra a kindred spirit, with the same kind of intense drive and ambition for power as he had. Cleopatra in turn saw in Julius Caesar her one chance to regain the throne. Thus an instant bond was formed. Caesar agreed to help return Cleopatra to the throne, but it was not merely a favor he was granting her. A tightly controlled Egypt meant fewer problems for Rome, and Caesar knew that Cleopatra would rule with a much firmer hand than her younger brother.

At the time, however, both Cleopatra and Caesar were essentially prisoners in the palace in Alexandria, since only a small force of Roman guards was available to defend them. When young Ptolemy XIII came before Caesar and learned that his sister was with him, he reportedly tore the crown from his head and ran out of the room, declaring that his cause had been betrayed. News of Cleopatra's presence in Caesar's chambers spread quickly throughout the population, and crowds began gathering outside the palace in protest.

Ptolemy was seized by Caesar's troops, and Caesar publicly read Ptolemy XII's will. He proposed that Cleopatra and Ptolemy XIII resume joint rule of Egypt and offered to return control of Cyprus to them, under the rule of Cleopatra's younger sister Arsinoë. When Ptolemy XIII's regents heard of

Cleopatra's restoration, however, they assembled troops and attempted to storm the palace, despite the young king's protestations.

During an elaborate and wildly extravagant feast celebrating the reconciliation of Cleopatra with Ptolemy XIII, Caesar received word that two of Ptolemy's regents, Achillas and Pothinus, had hatched a plot to assassinate him. He immediately had Pothinus killed, but Achillas escaped and had his forces attempt to capture Caesar's ships in the harbor. Caesar ordered the ships burned, secured Pharos Island, and sent for reinforcements.

Meanwhile, Cleopatra's sister Arsinoë, unhappy with Caesar's offer of Cyprus, allied herself with Achillas and his troops. Before long, however, the two were in conflict and Arsinoë arranged to have Achillas killed. She placed her own regent, Ganymede, in charge of Achillas's troops. It was weeks before Caesar's reinforcements arrived, but in March 47 B.C. they attacked the Egyptian fleet and swarmed the causeway leading to Pharos Island. The Egyptians were clever, though, and managed to surround the Romans by landing behind them. With no other way out, Caesar's troops were forced to swim for their ships from the island.

Caesar knew what he had to do. He released Ptolemy XIII, knowing that he would join forces with Ganymede and Arsinoë. With additional reinforcements, Caesar stormed Egypt and thoroughly defeated its army. Ptolemy XIII drowned in an attempt to escape the Romans. His body washed up on the shores of Alexandria still clad in the golden royal armor that he believed would protect him from harm.

The triumphant Roman troops once more marched through the streets of the city, and this time Cleopatra shared the glory. Accepting defeat, the Egyptian people welcomed Caesar and Cleopatra.

Julius Caesar was the Roman dictator, general, conqueror, who enormously influenced the history of western civilization. In 46 B.C. Caesar ruled the entire Roman Empire. He saw to it that the rickety and outmoded ways of Roman government were speedily reformed. However, Caesar chose not to place much emphasis on the public's opinion.

She was recrowned and assumed the throne with her youngest brother, who at 11 years old became Ptolemy XIV. Once more, according to custom, Cleopatra married her brother—but the youngster had no strong backers and presented no threat to her authority. Arsinoë, who had sided with Ptolemy XIII, was banished to Rome.

Caesar was now the uncontested ruler of the Roman Empire, and Cleopatra, who effectively ruled Egypt alone, seemed destined for greatness. While still in Alexandria, Caesar was treated by his lover to a triumphant and lavish excursion up the Nile River in a huge pleasure barge. The spectacular scene has been recreated in numerous movie and television accounts of Cleopatra's life. As Roman troops marched along the river banks, the royal barge, constructed of cedar, cypress, and gold and said to measure 300 feet long, sailed in majestic splendor. It contained banquet rooms, gardens, and courtyards. Banks of slaves gently pushed the floating palace through the waters. Egyptians along the shore were transfixed by the spectacle. There, in total control, rode Cleopatra, queen of Egypt, and Julius Caesar, who was fast becoming king of the Mediterranean world.

Caesar and Cleopatra knew that he could not stay in Alexandria. He was still married to Calpurnia, and more important, he had vowed to lead the Roman Empire into a new era of power and prosperity. He could only do that from the seat of power in Rome itself. He was also keenly aware that the threat of civil war—a seething conflict between Rome's old military guard and the new—was still very real in Rome.

In June 47 B.C., Caesar left Cleopatra, leaving behind three Roman legions to guard the queen. Some months later, according to Plutarch, Cleopatra bore a son, whom she named Caesarion ("young Caesar"). Although the year of Caesarion's birth is disputed—some historians believe that he was actually born two or more years later—Cleopatra claimed that the child was Caesar's, and Caesar himself never denied that he was the father. The queen even had a commemorative coin struck upon the child's birth, which depicted her as the goddess Isis holding her child, Horus-Caesarion (in the Egyptian religion, Horus was the son of Isis and Osiris).

Despite the threat of civil war, when Caesar left Alexandria he did not go directly to Rome. Pharnaces II of Asia Minor had long wanted to regain the territories his father had lost to the Romans decades earlier. With unrest in Rome and with Caesar in Egypt, Pharnaces decided that the time was ripe. Earlier that year, Pharnaces had defeated one of Caesar's best officers in battle, and then went on a rampage, slaughtering Roman citizens and mutilating young men and boys.

Caesar could not let these horrors go unpunished. In a five-day battle at Zela in Asia Minor, he soundly defeated Pharnaces with vastly superior forces. Pharnaces had foolishly ordered his men and chariots to charge up a hill toward Caesar's army, but the Romans quite handily charged down the hill and slaughtered the enemy before they could inflict much harm. Although Pharnaces survived the battle, he was later killed by his own men.

Caesar evidently saw the fight as trivial and almost beneath his dignity. It was after this battle that he made his famous clipped report—"Veni, Vidi, Vici" ("I came, I saw, I conquered). Four months after leaving Alexandria, he arrived in Rome and set about putting the city's affairs in order. He returned Cicero, an old but powerful enemy, to a position of importance. Marc Antony had been left in charge by Caesar, but because he was accused of dipping his hand into public funds to repay personal debts, Caesar banished him from public office for two years.

At the end of 47 B.C., Caesar once more left Rome to go to war. This time he headed for Thaspus, a north African coastal town in present-day Tunisia. There Cato, Caesar's longtime enemy in the senate, two of Pompey's sons, and a former trusted general amassed a huge force of 80,000 foot soldiers, 15,000 cavalry, and 100 "war elephants" to challenge Caesar. It was the most powerful opposition Caesar had ever faced in his military career.

At Thaspus, however, Caesar fulfilled his legacy as one of the greatest of all military generals. Leading mostly new and inexperienced soldiers who were

The demise of the Roman Empire still was in the distant future during Cleopatra's time. In this bas-relief, however, we see the Romans battling the barbarians. The barbarians were the tribes of Northern Europe, such as the Gauls.

vastly outnumbered, he tricked his opponents into dividing their forces, thereby weakening them, and slaughtered the enemy. A disgraced Cato fell on his own sword and killed himself rather than face defeat.

Julius Caesar returned to Rome in July 46 B.C. as dictator of the Roman Empire. To honor him, the city staged four spectacular and triumphant parades, the likes of which even extravagant Rome had never seen. Elaborately decorated floats depicted his war victories as columns of soldiers, thousands of musicians, and honored priests followed. Captured prisoners were paraded in chains, including Vercingetorix, whom Caesar had defeated years before in Gaul and had deliberately kept alive for an occasion to humiliate him. Caesar later ordered Vercingetorix to be executed. Another prize captive was Cleopatra's sister, Arsinoë, who was also dragged through the streets of Rome in chains—but so many Romans protested the cruel treatment of the teenager that Caesar spared her life and instead banished her to a religious temple.

The most astounding display amid the splendor of the parades was Cleopatra, the newly recrowned queen of Egypt. At Caesar's invitation, she had traveled with Ptolemy XIII and her son, Caesarion, to Rome. Egypt's royal family was housed in a magnificent villa on the banks of the Tiber River, courtesy of Caesar himself. The Romans were appalled. This was scandalous behavior—Julius Caesar was still married, after all. They were even more shocked when Caesar dedicated a new temple and placed within it a specially commissioned statue of Cleopatra. As a further honor, Caesar officially recognized Cleopatra as a member of his family.

Caesar seemed not to care whether his subjects objected to his behavior and his treatment of Cleopatra. However, he proved to be an able administrator. Among his many reforms was the adoption of the so-called Julian calendar—a change from the confusing Roman calendar that allowed for "leap years" and kept the days of the months more aligned with the annual seasons. (The Gregorian calendar, which we use today, replaced the Julian calendar in 1582 A.D.) Caesar also used his power to revamp what he viewed as a slow and inefficient government, and he plowed ahead with the reforms regardless of the consequences.

Although many admired Caesar's courage and military skill, they also feared his ruthless nature and powerful ambition. Their fears intensified when a rumor spread through Rome that Caesar intended to crown himself king. Romans viewed a kingship with horror—the last king had ruled four centuries earlier. But the rumor seemed to have truth to it. If it weren't true, they reasoned, then why was Cleopatra, the queen of Egypt, being received so warmly? And why did she wield so much influence over Caesar? They feared he planned to make himself king, divorce his wife, and rule the combined empires of Rome and Egypt with Cleopatra.

Caesar heard the rumors and tried to squelch them, but a plan was already taking shape among his subjects. When the emperor announced that he was launching a new military campaign in the east in March 44 B.C., Roman leaders decided they'd had enough. Gaius Cassius and Marcus Brutus, two Roman senators, led 60 of their fellow senators in a plot to assassinate Julius Caesar.

Cassius, the chief instigator of the plot, had been a general under Pompey and had fought against Caesar. He was married to Brutus's sister. Cassius had long felt that he had been unfairly treated by Caesar. Brutus was a scholarly man and a longtime friend of Caesar, but since the emperor had conducted a long affair with Brutus's mother, some speculated that Brutus may have been Caesar's son.

It is said that a soothsayer warned Caesar to "beware the Ides of March," but Caesar ignored the warning. Three days before Caesar was to leave for the eastern campaign, on March 15—the Ides of March—Caesar entered the senate room with Marc Antony. According to plan, one of the senators detained Antony just outside the senate while Caesar entered. The conspirators knew that Antony would attempt to defend Caesar.

As Caesar walked to his chair before the assembly, all the members rose to their feet, and the conspirators circled Caesar as though they were asking for favors,

which was not an unusual occurrence. Suddenly, one of them reached out a hand and pulled Caesar's royal purple robe from his shoulder. That was the cue—a symbolic act that signified that, having taken the physical trappings of his authority, they would now take his life.

The first blow struck Caesar from behind, a stab that pierced his shoulder. As he turned in surprise, the blows began to come from all sides. Again and

The Ides of March (March 15) was the day of Caesar's assassination on the Senate floor of the Roman Forum. Among those 60 men involved in the assassination plot was his close friend Brutus.

again his enemies stabbed him in growing fury, while Caesar tried vainly to defend himself with his bare fists. As the other senators in the chamber looked on in horror, Rome's greatest general sank slowly to the chamber floor, his white toga splattered with his own blood. Legend says that just before he died he looked up at his longtime friend, Brutus, who stood before him with a dagger in his hands, and asked, "Et tu, Brute?" ("You too, Brutus?") Caesar could not believe that he had been betrayed by one of his oldest and most trusted friends.

At Caesar's funeral, Marc Antony delivered a stirring tribute to his emperor, all the while holding aloft the bloody cloak Caesar was wearing when he was killed. We do not know what Antony said, but in the play *Julius Caesar*, written around 1599, William Shakespeare imagined a tribute that is still commonly recited today. "Friends, Romans, countrymen, lend me your ears," Shakespeare's Antony says. "I come to bury Caesar, not to praise him." Whatever Marc Antony really said, the speech so inflamed the Roman audience that many of the conspirators fled the city in fear. Instead of the peace that they had envisioned, the assassination of Julius Caesar brought a decade of intense strife to Rome. "We have removed the tyrant," said Cicero, a longtime enemy of Caesar's, "but the tyranny still lives." Cassius and Brutus later died by their own hands, and thousands of Romans were executed.

History does not record Cleopatra's reaction when she received news of Caesar's death. Surely, though, she must have felt as though her world had ended. In a way, it had—aside from the romantic relationship between Caesar and Cleopatra, it was now clear that her position as queen of Egypt was once again in jeopardy. Even more ominous, her very life was in danger. Rome did not look with favor upon this intruder from another land.

Cleopatra was a practical and level-headed woman, however. She had no time for mourning. Taking advantage of the chaos that swept the city after Caesar's death, she boarded a ship bound for Alexandria with Ptolemy XIV and Caesarion. The queen of Egypt would have to look elsewhere to protect her right to the throne.

Marc Antony met Cleopatra around 43-44 B.C. They shared a mutually gratifying union: she needed the Roman protection of her throne, and he would gain Egyptian wealth for himself and his troops. Cleopatra orchestrated a grand entrance on her floating palace for her first encounter with Marc Antony—her second successful seduction of a powerful Roman.

4

ANTONY AND CLEOPATRA

Julius Caesar was dead and Cleopatra still ruled Egypt, but how secure was her power without him? The three legions of Roman soldiers he had left in Alexandria still remained, but she did not know how long she would have their protection. Once again, the queen, now 25 years old, was forced to reexamine her situation.

Obviously, the answer to her problems still rested in Rome. But the empire was in turmoil, and she did not know who held power or who would become its next leader. Whose aid could she seek? While Cleopatra waited for the outcome of the power struggle in Rome, she took steps to secure her own position by apparently ordering the death of her brother and husband, Ptolemy XIV, who was poisoned shortly after their return to Alexandria. The queen would take no chances that another brother would become a rival for the throne.

In Rome, meanwhile, one man quickly tried to assume power—39-year-old Marc Antony, Caesar's longtime lieutenant and friend. Like Caesar, Antony had been born to a noble family. A handsome and athletic man, Antony was also a fine public speaker and a highly capable soldier. His mother, Julia, saw to his education and moral upbringing. When Antony was nine years old, his father, Marcus, was called to military duty in the Mediterranean, where pirates had been causing havoc with Roman shipping and trade. Rather than kill the pirates, Marcus used his influence to extort money and goods from coastal residents to the point where he became almost as threatening to the local residents as the pirates themselves. Finally, two years after his arrival, he was forced to engage the pirates in battle, but he was so soundly beaten that he died in disgrace in Crete in 71 B.C. Antony's mother remarried, but his new stepfather took little notice of the young man, who began to wander the streets of Rome with a wild, pleasure-seeking crowd. Before long Marc Antony was deeply in debt from his excessive drinking and gambling. In 58 B.C., when Antony was 25, he left for Greece to study oratory, which he believed he would need to pursue a political career—although some speculate that he was just as anxious to flee his creditors in Rome.

In Greece, Antony took part in the frequent military exercises that the local Roman forces conducted, and before long he earned a reputation for quick thinking and athletic gracefulness. When the Roman general Aulus Gabinius invited Antony to become a cavalry commander, his life took new direction. A participant in numerous victories, he joined Caesar's army in Gaul after Gabinius was ordered back to Rome on accusation of extortion. Antony became Caesar's dependable aide.

At the time, Caesar was facing a full-scale revolt of the Gallic tribes, led by the nobleman Vercingetorix (Caesar would parade this enemy through the streets of Rome during his triumphal march six years later.) Antony received many honors for his efforts against the Gauls, and was rewarded by being promoted to Caesar's second-in-command.

In 48 B.C., while Caesar was fighting Pompey in Africa, Antony was left in charge over Italy. He grew bored with this rather peaceful duty, however, and eventually he resorted to his youthful habits of heavy drinking, gambling, and other questionable kinds of behavior. It wasn't long before he was once again heavily in debt, reportedly took public funds, and made a frequent public spectacle of himself. Such displays by a Roman officer greatly displeased Caesar, who heard news of his second-in-command's behavior and promptly removed Antony from office. After the general returned home, Antony vowed to reform, paid off his debts, and did away with his episodes of mis-behavior. Before long he was back in favor with Caesar.

This would not be the last time Marc Antony displayed such lapses in behavior, however. Whenever he was not occupied with a political crisis or with military matters, he seemed to revert to corrupt, cruel, and wanton behavior. Despite these flaws, Antony received the loyalty of Caesar's troops after the emperor's assassination. With this backing and the rank of consul, Antony took control of the Roman senate.

Antony had not counted on Caesar's will, however. In it, the general had named his 18-year-old grand-nephew and adopted son, Octavian, as his heir. A rather sickly youth, Octavian was regarded by Antony as little more than an annoyance—and hardly a threat to his power. But he had greatly underestimated the youth. While Antony was in Gaul to quiet a political distur-bance, Octavian arrived in Rome. Renaming himself Gaius Julius Caesar, he quickly befriended Antony's political enemies, including the great orator Cicero. With the help of Cicero and the senate, Antony was officially declared an enemy of the state. In 43 B.C., Octavian led an army into Modena, where he over-threw Marc Antony.

But the defeat was temporary. Older and wiser by now, Antony forged new alliances with several Roman

The dashing commander was born into high Roman society. At the age of 25 he went to Greece to perfect his rhetoric skills. Marc Antony was known for his drunkenness and debauched youth before he chose to seriously pursue a military career.

generals, including Lepidus, who had once led Caesar's army. The turn of fortune caused Octavian in turn to reconsider his position. When the Senate refused him a consulship, Octavian decided to join Antony. Along with Lepidus, Octavian and Antony formed the Second Triumvirate in November 43 B.C. There followed a reign of terror, in which every enemy of the state—and every enemy of Antony, Octavian, and Lepidus—was tracked down and executed. Antony was particularly brutal to Cicero, who was beheaded and had his hands cut off before his corpse was put on public display. The following year, Antony distinguished himself in the battle of Philippi by defeating Caesar's conspirators. Everyone who had had even the slightest conflict with Caesar was eliminated.

The members of the Second Triumvirate divided the Roman territories among themselves: Lepidus took Spain; Octavian had Africa, Sardinia, and Sicily; and Antony took control of Gaul. His first goal was to raise funds for his own army, with which he would oversee the administration of his provinces. While in Tarsus, Asia Minor, Marc Antony summoned Cleopatra VII. He had heard rumors that Egypt's royals had aided Caesar's conspirators at Philippi.

Marc Antony's summons supplied the answer to Cleopatra's problem. He was now the most powerful man in Rome, and would secure her throne and protect Egypt if she won him over. In return, she could guarantee that Egypt's wealth and bounty would keep him and his armies well supplied. Cleopatra already knew a great deal about Antony. She had seen him on a number of occasions while she was a guest of Caesar's in Rome. She knew of his reputation as a man who enjoyed the company of many women, despite the fact that he was married. And Cleopatra, now 28 years old, was at the height of her beauty and still captivated others with her charm and wit.

The young queen began a campaign to capture Antony's attention. First, she decided to ignore his summons. Another came, and then a third. She ignored those also. When a fourth summons arrived, Cleopatra reasoned that Antony must either be highly curious or extremely angry—so she obeyed and went to see him.

According to all reports, the Egyptian queen made quite an entrance. Antony was camped along the river in the ancient city of Tarsus, when suddenly he spotted a huge barge that was so elaborate it seemed to be a floating palace. To the astonishment of the people gathered along the banks, Queen Cleopatra entered the city on a golden ship bedecked with sails made of purple silk. The music of flutes and harps drifted across the water as the silver oars of the slaves dipped silently into the water. Small boys dressed as angelic emissaries and carrying gigantic plumes fanned the air to prevent even a fly from disturbing the stately queen of Egypt. Cleopatra, costumed as Aphrodite, the Greek goddess of love and beauty, reclined on a couch beneath a canopy of woven gold in the center of the barge.

The spectacle was enough to bedazzle anyone. But if Antony was waiting for Cleopatra to meet him in the marketplace, he was disappointed. When he sent word that he wished her to come ashore for an evening meal, she refused. Instead, Cleopatra asked him and his friends aboard the ship that evening. Intrigued, Antony accepted.

When he arrived on board the barge, the tables were set with golden plates and jeweled drinking cups. Tiny torches fixed in the ship's rigging created a picture of intoxicating beauty and excitement. The deck of the barge was carpeted with rose petals. No one knows whether Antony ever questioned Cleopatra about aiding his enemies. By the end of the evening, however, he was smitten with the Egyptian queen.

Some historians doubt Antony's love for Cleopatra. It is true that he enjoyed the company of many women, but Cleopatra was unlike any of them. Aside from her beauty and power, she was reportedly a fascinating companion—witty, intelligent, flirtatious, and extremely well-spoken. So overwhelmed was Marc Antony that some Romans claimed she had cast a spell on him and denounced her as a witch. Did Cleopatra truly love Marc Antony in return? It appears so. By all accounts she was faithful to him, just as she had been to Caesar. Certainly the two depended heavily upon each other, not only for affection but also for protection and power.

Antony spent the winter of 41 to 40 B.C. with Cleopatra in Alexandria. Reports say that the couple did little during those months but engage in "debauchery and folly." Antony's baser habits, his heavy drinking, gambling, bawdy behavior, and womanizing, seem to have reasserted themselves. It was said that on occasion he led Cleopatra and other friends down back streets of Alexandria disguised as a rowdy gang of commoners. Whatever she thought of this behavior, Cleopatra participated in such escapades to keep Antony interested and to insure that he remained loyal to her.

Politically, the two rulers forged an alliance in which

The Gallic Nobleman Vercingatorix, who would later be captured and executed by Caesar, is depicted in this 19th-century original by Royer. It was at the time of Vercingatorix's Gallic revolt that Marc Antony joined Caesar's military forces. In a short time, he would become Caesar's second in command.

Cleopatra agreed to supply Antony with any military supplies he might require for future wars; he was also given complete access to Egypt's great shipbuilding business. In return, Antony put the considerable power of Rome behind Cleopatra's throne. He also gave her the island of Cyprus as an Egyptian territory. Not quite satisfied, Cleopatra made one more request. She asked that her sister Arsinoë, whose life had been spared by Caesar, be put to death. Antony complied. Now, no siblings remained left to challenge the queen for the throne of Egypt.

In the year 40 B.C., two pieces of alarming news reached Antony in Alexandria. His wife, Fulvia, herself an ambitious woman, had joined forces with Antony's brother Lucius and had declared war against Octavian. In addition, Rome's eastern enemy, Parthia, was in turmoil. Reluctantly, Antony departed Egypt and left Cleopatra behind. Later that year, Cleopatra gave birth to twins, whom she named Alexander Helios and Cleopatra Selene. Antony and Cleopatra would not see one another again for three years.

After Antony's departure for Rome, Cleopatra made what was apparently a rare error in judgement, when she antagonized Herod, the wealthy and powerful king of Judea (modern-day Israel), who is noted in the Bible as having been in power at Christ's birth. Cleopatra wanted Herod's territory; it was the only part of the old Ptolemaic dynasty that she did not control. When she requested that Antony turn it over to her, he refused. The two men were longtime friends, but Antony also knew that he might one day need Herod's military support. Still, he ceded a portion of Jericho, over which Herod also ruled, to Egypt in an effort to appease Cleopatra. In the end, the transaction created a rift between the thrones of Egypt and Judea that would ultimately prove costly, both to Antony and to Cleopatra.

Troops that had once held allegiance to Julius Caesar gave their loyalty to Marc Antony after their former leader was brutally assassinated. In this marble relief carving found in Ephesus, Turkey, a battle scene between Parthians and Romans is immortalized.

By the time Antony reached Rome in 40 B.C., his wife and brother had been defeated by Octavian. Fulvia died soon after, and Antony and Octavian once again settled their differences and reaffirmed the Second Triumvirate. When they redivided the empire, however, Lepidus lost a great deal of power and influence: he was given only minor provinces in

Africa. Antony, by contrast, now controlled the entire eastern empire and Octavian the west, with the Ionian Sea as a dividing line. As part of this new agreement, Antony consented to take Octavian's half-sister, Octavia, as his fourth wife.

Although marriages of political convenience were common in Rome, the news could not have pleased Cleopatra. Antony undoubtedly agreed to the union for two reasons: first, Octavian would be less likely to ally himself against Antony if he were married to his sister; second, the Roman public, which intensely disliked Cleopatra because of her previous affair with Julius Caesar, would be pleased by the marriage and more amenable to his rule.

Antony now turned his attention to Rome's most dangerous foe, Parthia. He set about preparing to do battle. Before the battle, which was launched in 36 B.C., he met Cleopatra in Antioch, Syria, and there, on the Orontes River, the two were married. The fact that Antony was already married seems to have made little difference. This union was obviously not recognized in Rome, but it was accepted in the eastern part of the empire and in Egypt. In addition, it legitimized the twins born to Cleopatra. Sometime later, Antony and Cleopatra's third child was born, a son named Ptolemy Philadelphus.

From Antioch, Antony went to battle against Parthia—a war that proved not only costly, but politically disastrous. On the battlefield, it seemed clear, Marc Antony was no Julius Caesar. Despite the fact that he had amassed what was probably the largest Roman army to that time, he unwisely fragmented his troops and thus lost half of them while gaining no ground. Some historians speculate that he was simply in too great a hurry to return to Cleopatra, who met him on the Mediterranean with fresh supplies, and that he was distracted from the important details of military strategy.

Perhaps to boost his ego after the defeat, Antony focused his attention on the minor kingdom of Armenia, whose king he captured in 34 B.C. Antony could have followed the custom of taking a vanquished ruler to Rome, where the defeated leader was displayed before its citizens. This action would likely have restored some of his lost prestige. Instead, Antony ignored the custom and brought the Armenian king to Cleopatra's feet in Alexandria.

If Roman citizens were stunned by this insult against tradition, they were no doubt speechless when they heard what transpired next in Egypt's capital city. To celebrate Antony's overblown triumph in Armenia, Cleopatra held a massive feast in the great gymnasium of the city, which some now referred to as New Rome. Dressed as the goddess Isis, Cleopatra sat high above her subjects with Antony, garbed as the Greek god Dionysius, by her side on a golden throne atop a silver dais. Slightly below them, on smaller thrones, sat the couple's three children and Caesarion, now 13 years old. Antony formally recognized the teen as the true son of Caesar—a declaration guaranteed to infuriate Octavian.

During the festival, Antony also declared his Egyptian wife the Queen of Kings. Along with Caesarion, she was named ruler of Cyprus, Libya, Syria, and Egypt. (The coinage that was struck to mark the occasion, however, does not include Caesarion; rather, it portrays Cleopatra as absolute monarch.) Antony also named their three children rulers of various eastern provinces, even though the youngest was just two years old. These eastern lands, which came to be known as the "donations of Alexandria," were given to Cleopatra and her children to recognize Cleopatra's position as heir to the dynasty of the Ptolemies. Romans were furious over the gift.

Marc Antony and Cleopatra as seen in this original painting by Trevisoni were known for their extravagant lifestyle and pursuit of luxuries. At their first dinner together, the couple dined on gold plates and sipped wine from jeweled cups as flutes played.

Beauty in the Ancient World

Cleopatra is commonly depicted wearing exotic, striking gold jewelry, but she is most famous for her pearls. These gems were very popular in ancient times. Caesar himself collected them because, it is said, he liked the feel of them in his hand. The Roman author Pliny the Elder wrote that Cleopatra had two pearls that were the "largest of all time." Another story tells of Cleopatra ordering a cup of vinegar during a banquet, dropping one of her pearl earrings into the cup, and drinking the vinegar after the pearl had dissolved, to the astonishment of Antony. The story is highly improbable—pearls do not dissolve in vinegar—but the tale has often been told to emphasize the Egyptian queen's reckless extravagance and her lavish beauty.

Cleopatra would also have used cosmetics to enhance her features. A popular cosmetic material was henna, a vegetable dye used to color hair and to stain nails, palms, and the soles of the feet a reddish hue. To tint the lips and eyelids, women used minerals ground into powder. For cheek color, they used seaweed and other plants; white lead powder was sometimes applied to the skin to lighten it. Ancient Egyptian and Greek women had used cosmetics long before Cleopatra's time, and she was probably elaborately made up for her first meeting with Marc Antony. An ancient book on such materials has even been attributed to Cleopatra, although it is doubtful that she was the author.

Cleopatra, now 35, had achieved her dream of restoring the Ptolemaic dynasty to its former glory and of regaining absolute power over Egypt. Her empire now very nearly matched in size that which had been held by Ptolemy II. With Antony's protection and support, she knew that she would restore the full honor of her ancestors.

In just four years, however, this union between Antony and Cleopatra—whether forged out of love, a desire for power, or both—would end in disaster. The marriage and the political alliance between the two rulers would ultimately destroy not only them, but also the very stability of the world as they knew it. Cleopatra lived, worked, schemed, planned, even murdered in order to insure that Egypt's years of glory, culture, and prosperity would continue for eons. Instead, she would go down in history as the last of the Ptolemy line.

Octavian, Julius Caesar's designated heir would later be crowned Emperor Augustus. He became Marc Antony's enemy in the power struggle for control of Rome. Octavian began his personal war against Marc Antony by revealing the contents of Marc Antony's will that highly favored the Egyptian Queen, infuriating the Roman people.

5

THE TRAGEDY OF ACTIUM

ntony and Cleopatra both realized that a battle with Octavian seemed inevitable. There could be no compromise between the two men: both craved the undisputed leadership of the Roman Empire. Antony may have underestimated Octavian's political and military skills, but he did understand his ultimate goal, because it was the same as his own. He did not realize, however, that the younger man had learned much since their last encounter, and had managed to turn the Roman people against Antony. It had not been difficult: Antony had severely misjudged the Roman people's anger over the honors he bestowed on Cleopatra, and they were ripe for revolt. Their outrage only escalated when Antony divorced his Roman wife, Octavia, in 32 B.C. Upon the edict, 400 senators who had supported Antony now turned against him.

Public opinion was further inflamed when Octavian obtained a copy of what he claimed was Marc Antony's will. It was customary for a Roman leader to deposit a copy of his will with the vestal virgins, priestesses who served the state for 30-year periods, during which time they vowed to remain pure and to perform certain state duties. (They were buried alive if they violated their vow of chastity.) Although the content of one's will was supposed to remain private, Octavian seized a copy of Antony's and divulged its supposed contents to members of the senate. A master at swaying public opinion, Octavian fomented a particularly fierce anger over the clause stating that his body should be returned to Cleopatra in Egypt, regardless of where he died.

With Rome on the brink of civil war, Antony and Cleopatra traveled to Ephesus, Greece, to devise a plan. There, Cleopatra promised Antony part of the excellent Egyptian fleet, including supply ships. She opened the Egyptian treasury to furnish him with enough funds to equip a vast military force. So committed were the two rulers to one another's fortunes that when Antony's advisors suggested that the war would be better waged were the queen returned to Egypt, Antony refused to dismiss her.

Cleopatra had no intention of standing by while Antony waged war. After all, she was paying for a good part of his effort, and she needed to be sure that Egypt was protected. But Antony's refusal to send her back to Egypt caused a dilemma. The senators who remained loyal to Antony believed that Octavian was unprepared for an all-out war, and they advised a swift invasion of Italy while the younger ruler was still gathering his forces. Moreover, they argued, Antony was better prepared to fight on land than at sea, and he was a better land general than Octavian. Antony would gain favor from the Romans if he won the battle with Octavian over the Italian territories.

But if the Romans viewed Cleopatra as a co-leader of Antony's campaign, he risked alienating his own generals and other military leaders allied with him. Antony could not move with Cleopatra, yet he would not move without her. There was one option open to him—he would launch the battle at sea, a strategy that Cleopatra favored. It was here, perhaps, that the battle was lost before it was even fought.

In the fall of 32 B.C., Antony and Cleopatra settled for the winter in Patrae on the Gulf of Corinth in Greece. Patrae was part of a chain of towns that functioned as supply links for goods coming from Egypt. The following spring, they moved their head-quarters, most of their army, and the fleet to Actium, a splendid harbor city on the southern shore of the Gulf of Ambracia.

Antony was confident. His forces, both ground and naval, were larger than Octavian's, and his anchorage at Actium seemed perfect. But what looked to be an excellent haven for Antony's fleet turned out to be disastrous. Antony had not counted on the military skills of Octavian's exceedingly talented admiral, Agrippa. With lightning speed, Agrippa seized strategic naval positions along Antony's defenses, cutting off his supply lines to Egypt. The perfect haven had become a perfect trap.

Antony tried to free his forces by drawing Octavian into battle—but Octavian refused to engage. Time and the Grecian summer heat were on his side. Months passed in a stalemate, as Antony's navy remained locked in the gulf with no means of obtaining supplies or replacements. Fresh water was scarce, and soon disease began spreading through Antony's camps. Soldiers, including some of Antony's best generals, began to desert. The situation grew desperate. By late August, Antony knew that he had to break free of the trap Octavian set or surrender completely.

Antony's advisors disagreed on an effective strategy. His senior officers argued for abandoning the fleet and trying to cut through Macedonia to Egypt using ground forces. But Cleopatra still trusted the sea. She did not believe that Octavian could defeat such a massive armada. In the end, Antony agreed with her.

Antony and Cleopatra's armada was indeed enormous: his original fleet numbered 500 warships and several hundred merchant vessels. He had perhaps 70,000 foot soldiers and 12,000 cavalrymen, and he was backed by Cleopatra's fleet of 60 warships. The queen herself would sail on her flagship Antonias, which carried her war chest of gold, silver, and jewels. Perhaps the most powerful fleet ever seen in the ancient world, the Roman armada must have been an awesome sight. Each warship was a massive floating fort with up to 10 rowers assigned to each oar to provide explosive power during naval maneuvers. Timbers bound with iron spikes protected the sides of the ships, and archers stood atop the ships' towers, poised to rain flaming arrows down upon the enemy. A great bronze beak that protruded from the prow of each vessel was used for ramming other ships and crippling them so that the warriors could incapacitate their enemies and board and capture their ships.

For all its power, however, Antony's fleet was slow and difficult to maneuver. In addition, many of his men had been newly recruited and hastily and poorly trained. By the time of the actual battle, Antony's forces had suffered so much illness and so many desertions that he could equip only 230 of his 500 ships for fighting.

Opposing Antony was Octavian's slightly larger force of about 100,000 foot soldiers, 12,000 cavalrymen, and 400 warships. More important than the numbers, however, was the size and swiftness of Octavian's fleet. His warships were easier to handle, even by inexperienced crews.

The Battle of Actium began on September 2, a clear, sunny, windy day in 31 B.C. Although the conflict itself was brief—in fact, it is not even considered a major sea battle—the events that followed sealed its place in history as a turning point for the ancient world. At dawn, Antony positioned his fleet in a line at the mouth of the gulf, with his strongest squadrons at each end of the line. Behind the center of the line were

Cleopatra's 60 warships. Opposing them, and farther out to sea, were Octavian's forces under the command of Agrippa. The armies of both Antony and Octavian watched from the shore.

For a brief period, the warriors waited anxiously to see how the wind would turn. Confident that they could easily overpower the enemy's smaller ships, Antony's men grew impatient. Finally the winds retreated, and Antony led his fleet into the middle of the gulf, spreading them out in a longer line that stretched for more than a mile.

The battle began around noon. Octavian knew that he had to avoid being rammed by Antony's heavy-prowed ships, so he ordered his small ships to dart around the enemy forces, firing flaming arrows and catapult shots as they passed. In return, Antony's archers, high in their perches, showered their enemy with fiery spears.

For a time, the forces were at a standoff. It soon became obvious, however, that Antony's bulky ships were no match for the lighter and more mobile fleet of Octavian. His own flagship in flames, Antony escaped to another vessel. Just then, a heavy breeze sprang up from the opposite direction, forcing the oarsmen to row harder than ever and slowing the bigger ships even more. Many of Antony's vessels were trapped and burned as a result.

While Marc Antony paced the deck in fury as he directed the fight, the center of the long line of warships began to weaken. Finally, it broke, and through the breach appeared Cleopatra's flagship, its purple sails unfurled, followed by the rest of her fleet.

But Cleopatra's ships did not come to Antony's rescue as he expected. Instead, all 60 ships headed for the mouth of the gulf and the safety of Egypt. The Egyptian forces, it seemed, were deserting Antony.

Quickly, Antony boarded a faster vessel and caught up with Cleopatra's flagship, with about 40 of his ships following him. To the utter surprise and dismay of Antony's forces, their commander-in-chief boarded Cleopatra's ship and fled with her, deserting his armada. It is difficult to imagine what Antony's soldiers must have felt as they watched their leader run from battle.

Antony's forces bravely fought on without their leader, but there was no hope. By nightfall the battle was over and Octavian was victorious. Fifteen of Antony's mighty warships had been burned, sunk, or captured, and more than 5,000 of his soldiers were killed.

Why did Cleopatra and Marc Antony lose the Battle of Actium? Did they suffer defeat because they ran away? Were their actions a result of cowardice on Antony's part or ruthlessness on Cleopatra's part? The historian Plutarch, who wrote a biography of Marc Antony 100 years later, certainly believed it was the former. It is clear that most of Rome in the aftermath of the battle believed the same. Plutarch described Antony as a man who could no longer think for himself, but who was instead compelled to accede to the will of his beloved queen.

Other accounts disagree. It is far more likely, they assert, that Cleopatra and Antony had discussed the possibility of defeat before the battle even began, and had planned the getaway should defeat appear likely. An escape with Egypt's war chest intact aboard the queen's flagship, with all of her warships and 40 of Antony's, and with 20,000 troops, would allow both rulers to fight another day. The fact that the fleet carried sails also lends credence to the idea that they had pre-planned a quick getaway: ordinarily, warships relied solely on their rowers because the weight of sails made the ships difficult to control in the heat of battle. But when Antony's ship captains requested that they leave behind their sails for the fight, Antony ordered them to take them aboard, using the excuse that they might need the sails to pursue and capture the enemy's lighter ships.

In the aftermath of the escape, Cleopatra seemed to react to the flight from Actium as though it had been carefully planned. She looked forward to another military encounter with Octavian. But Marc Antony could not live with what he had done. Even if the flight seemed like good strategy at the time, even if it did save them for another fight, Antony had deserted his men. Even as he boarded Cleopatra's flagship, he seemed aware of the enormity of his actions. He brooded over his act of cowardice and refused to speak to Cleopatra

Map showing the area ensconced in the Battle of Actium. The battle itself occurred on September 2, 31 B.C. and would at once cement Octavian's ruling position in the Roman Empire. It would also end Marc Antony's formerly successful military and political career.

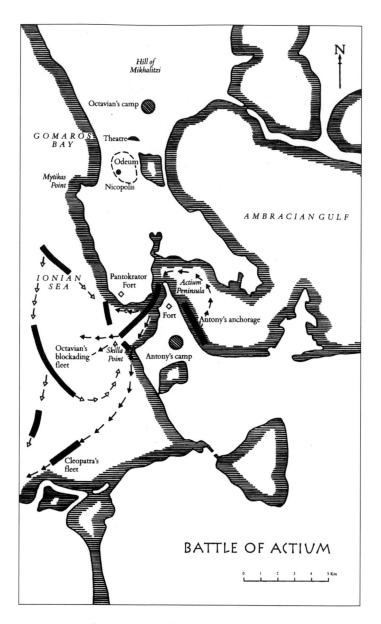

BATTLE OF ACTIUM

or anyone else. Instead, he sat in the prow of the ship, his head in his hands.

Antony did not return to Alexandria with Cleopatra. He went off alone into the desert, and when he finally returned to the city, he sequestered himself for months, speaking to no one—not even the queen herself. As for

Octavian, his next goal was, of course, to follow Antony and Cleopatra to Egypt and take them as prisoners. But he knew that this could wait—he was aware that Antony was now a broken man and no longer posed an immediate threat. Moreover, he was struggling with political troubles elsewhere. While many of the territories under the Roman Empire supported Octavian, some did not. In an effort to quell the unrest, he traveled to the Italian region to make peace. Additionally, Roman veterans were beginning to return home and were demanding the pay they had been promised for service in battle—funds that Octavian did not have. He had expected to take advantage of plunder from Egypt to pay for the costs.

Octavian needed months to equip another army to march into Egypt. He knew that he needed to pass through the eastern territories, which were still largely loyal to Antony. Herod of Judea quickly assured Octavian that he would not resist such an advance, however, and other leaders soon followed. The turn of fortune was Herod's revenge for Cleopatra's ill treatment of him. Those who remained loyal to Antony implored him to lead them against Octavian, but Antony no longer had the stomach for war. When he did not answer their pleas, they too joined Octavian, who continued marching toward Alexandria.

Marc Antony knew well that his reputation and his career were ruined. He would never succeed Caesar as Rome's leader. But while the Battle of Actium had left him shattered and defeated, Cleopatra still held onto her goal of ruling a vast and powerful empire, independent from the rule of Rome.

In this brightly illustrated 15th-century Italian manuscript Cleopatra's joys and struggles for her kingdom and for her lover, Marc Antony are shown in the various panels. At the top, Cleopatra meets with Octavian in Alexandria to beg for her future and her children's future roles in Egypt. To the lower left is a banquet with Marc Antony, and to the lower right she is shown mourning Marc Antony.

6

THE LAST OF THE PTOLEMIES

Antony finally returned to Cleopatra at her palace in Alexandria, and there they spent the last winter of their lives together. At first, Cleopatra pretended to have returned triumphant from the Battle of Actium, and she set about rebuilding her fleet and her army. She knew that the dream of a united Roman-Egyptian empire was lost, but she still had Egypt, and she meant to keep it by any means possible.

While Antony wallowed in despair, Cleopatra ordered most of her ships to be transported overland to the Red Sea. It was a huge and difficult feat, but she planned to be able to escape Octavian's forces should he attack from the west. She would have her treasury loaded onto the waiting ships at the Red Sea, and she and Antony could flee eastward with their children. Egypt, she determined, would survive to fight another day.

But Egypt's Arab neighbors, unhappy with its rule over them, exacted a fierce toll on the queen—they burned her ships stationed at the Red Sea. It was time to face the truth. Octavian was nearing Alexandria and no Roman forces stood in his way. Cleopatra's forces alone could not stop him. It might be impossible to fight Octavian, Cleopatra decided, but perhaps she could reason with him.

When Octavian landed at Phoenicia (modern-day Syria) in the summer of 30 B.C., he was met by emissaries from the Egyptian queen. Cleopatra's message was clear: she would vacate the throne if her son Caesarion, now age 16, was crowned king of Egypt. As for Antony, he asked only that he be allowed to live out his life quietly in Egypt. This was not an unusual request; Roman generals who lost in battle were often granted similar courtesies out of respect for their service to Rome.

In a deliberate affront, Octavian ignored Antony entirely and answered only the message from Cleopatra. His words were chilling: she could save herself and her kingdom if she expelled Antony from Egypt or executed him. Cleopatra would do neither—but knowing that her son's life was now threatened, she immediately sent him east, away from danger.

The Roman army was closing in. When word came that the advance guard was near the city, Antony suddenly roused himself. He took his men to meet the enemy force and managed to push the advance guard back. It was his last victory, and a meaningless one at that, yet Antony and Cleopatra staged a victory celebration that evening.

It is said that a strange, faint sound of flutes was heard throughout Alexandria that night. According to legend, the sound of flutes at night means that the gods are deserting a city just before it is about to fall. Regardless of the portent, Antony pledged to lead his remaining troops against Octavian in the morning, whatever the cost.

In the early hours of August 1, 30 B.C., Antony departed from the palace to face the Roman troops— but he was forced to watch in despair from a hilltop as his remaining fleet surrendered without a fight to Octavian. When his own cavalrymen followed suit, the general could do nothing but return to the palace in total defeat. He began to wonder whether even his beloved Cleopatra had betrayed him.

Cleopatra, meanwhile, had heard of the surrender and knew the end was near, so she barricaded herself in her monument [memorial building]. When Antony attempted to see her, he was told that the queen had committed suicide. Perhaps it was her choice of the monument as a refuge that helped to spread the rumor of the queen's death at her own hand. Horrified and broken, Marc Antony decided he could not face life without Cleopatra. He asked his servant Eros to kill him with his own sword. Eros could not, and instead killed himself to avoid having to deny his master. Antony felt he had no choice. In the Roman custom, he placed the point of his sword against his chest and fell upon it.

Marc Antony did not die immediately, however. When palace servants found him, they hoisted him on ropes through the window of the room where the queen was barricaded. It is said that Cleopatra grew hysterical upon learning that her beloved was dying, and she threw herself upon him, covering her own garments with his blood. According to Plutarch, Antony rallied briefly and requested some wine. Marc Antony died in the arms of Cleopatra at 51 years old.

After Antony's death, Cleopatra received another message from Octavian. Surrender, he said, and you will not be harmed. Cleopatra replied that she would leave her chamber only upon Octavian's word that her children would remain as rulers of Egypt. The messenger assured her that she could trust Octavian on this request.

But the queen of Egypt had not survived this long in her perilous world by foolishly believing such pledges. She suspected that Octavian would promise anything to get what he wanted. She believed that, perhaps even more than acquiring Egypt's riches, he wanted to return triumphantly to Rome with the queen in chains.

This illustration depicts the minutes following Marc Antony's suicide. Cleopatra reportedly blanketed her lover with her own body. The illustration is taken from a production of William Shakespeare's Antony and Cleopatra *performed at the Drury Lane Theatre in London.*

She knew that she would be a most prized and appreciated "gift" to the Roman citizens who despised her.

Accordingly, Cleopatra refused to surrender—so on the day after Antony's death, Octavian's soldiers broke into the monument and captured her. According to reports, they also prevented her from committing suicide. Octavian did allow his royal prisoner to leave her chamber, under heavy guard, for the elaborate funeral ceremony of Marc Antony.

For several days following the burial of Antony, Cleopatra refused all food and drink. But Octavian was not about to let the queen starve herself to death. He sent word that unless she began taking food, he would kill her children. The queen had no choice, and she began to eat. Later, Octavian visited Cleopatra in her chamber. There are many reports of what the queen said and did at that meeting, including a reminder to Octavian of her love for Caesar. She also offered to purchase the throne of Egypt for her son, using the country's vast treasures. Of course, Octavian had already seized all of Cleopatra's treasures and was assuming command of the kingdom. He refused her offers.

Around mid-August, Cleopatra was told that Octavian was preparing to leave for Rome, taking her and her children with him as his prisoners. With great heartache, she envisioned the spectacle she and her children would create for the Romans. Perhaps she thought about the day when her own sister, Arsinoë, was dragged through Rome's streets in chains at Caesar's request. But she was Cleopatra, Egypt's queen. If she could not fulfill her destiny to restore the glory of her ancestors, she was determined that she would at least die in a manner that honored their greatness.

Some reports say that by this time Octavian had changed his mind about presenting Cleopatra to Roman citizens as a royal prisoner. What seemed triumphant to him, he realized, was a base humiliation for the proud and once-powerful queen. But he could not risk sending her into exile instead, where she would likely plan to return to take the throne once more.

Whatever Octavian may have been thinking, he permitted Cleopatra to visit Antony's grave a final time. When she returned to her chamber, she wrote a letter to Octavian asking that her body be buried next to Antony's. She bathed, dressed, and ate a festive meal. Then, according to legend, she allowed herself to be bitten by an asp—a poisonous snake that had been smuggled into her chamber in a basket of figs by one of her servants.

When Octavian received the letter, he suspected that

Cleopatra was planning suicide and immediately dispatched soldiers to her chamber. It was too late. There lay the body of Cleopatra, the stately queen of Egypt, dressed in royal finery and lying on a bed of gold. Her servants lay dying at her feet. She was as impressive in death as she had been in life.

Although some historians question the legend of Cleopatra's death by a poisonous snake, it is the image of the dying queen that has been passed down through the centuries and the one with which we are most familiar today. Granting her last request, Octavian ordered that she be buried next to Antony in the royal tomb. The extraordinary Cleopatra VII, queen of Egypt, the last of the Ptolemies to rule, was dead at 39.

What happened to the great kingdom of Egypt? For nearly three weeks after the queen's death, the children of Cleopatra were, in name only, the rulers of Egypt. On August 31 of that year, Octavian declared himself pharaoh. After centuries of fighting to remain independent from Rome, Egypt became a Roman province. But though most Roman territories were placed under the governorship of the Roman senate, Octavian made a special exception for Egypt. He had no real interest in Egypt politically, except to use it to provide wealth for Rome, so the kingdom functioned in effect as his own personal property. It was governed by a prefect who reported directly to Octavian. Egypt's first governor under this new system was Cornelius Gallus.

Although Octavian exploited much of the eastern desert of Egypt for its mineral wealth, he did respect the memory of Alexander the Great by safeguarding and maintaining the city of Alexandria. A series of good administrators appointed by Octavian brought new prosperity to the land. Over the next few centuries, many Roman emperors were drawn to Egypt by the magnificent monuments of its ancient civilization. A number of Ptolemaic temples were completed well into the first century A.D., and other new buildings were

erected as well, such as the Isis temple at Deir es-Shelwit. In time, however, Egypt fell into decline, suffering from the many years of exploitation and heavy taxation by Rome.

When the Christian city of Constantinople was founded (324-30 A.D.) during the reign of Constantine I, Alexandria's importance as the great city of the East was diminished. In the seventh century A.D., Arabs invaded Egypt and transformed it over the following centuries into an Arabic-speaking state in which Islam was the predominant religion. Great Britain took over and occupied Egypt in 1882; in 1922 the country became a constitutional monarchy. Following a military coup in 1952, however, Gamal Abdel Nasser became the first native Egyptian ruler in more than 2,000 years.

Not long after Marc Antony's suicide, Cleopatra took her own life rather than suffer humiliation and/or execution at the hands of Octavian. She legendarily let herself be poisoned by an asp.

The Romans wasted no time in celebrating the defeat of Antony and Cleopatra. This coin commemorates this victory for Octavian and his empire; Octavian announced that he was Egypt's new Pharaoh on August 31, 30 B.C. He would place Cornelius Gallus there to act as his governor. Egypt would effectively become part of Octavian's personal property.

What became of Cleopatra's children? Soon after her death, her son Caesarion, age 17, was killed by order of Octavian, who was unwilling to risk being challenged by another relative of Caesar's. The twins and young Ptolemy were raised by Antony's widow, Octavia. Octavian had spared their lives because he thought them too young to pose a threat to him. The two boys apparently died of natural causes while still young. Cleopatra Selene, one of the twins, later married King Juba II of Numidia and Mauretania. Her own son's death in 40 A.D. marked the end of the long line of Ptolemies.

What of Octavian, the once sickly youth whom Antony had so badly misjudged and who now held the power of both Rome and Egypt? After he proclaimed himself ruler of Egypt in August 30 B.C., he became master of the entire Greco-Roman world. Three years later he became Rome's first emperor—named Augustus, or Caesar Augustus.

Augustus was an administrative genius. With great patience and skill, he built the Roman principate, a government system that enabled him to maintain total control. He created a superb network of roads and an efficient fleet to keep order. He consolidated the power of the empire in Rome itself and began the *Pax Romana* ("Roman Peace"), a period of relative calm throughout the Mediterranean, North Africa, and Persia that began with his concept that individual provinces could govern themselves as long as they accepted Roman military control and taxation. Additionally, the building program begun by Augustus launched a great transformation of Rome into the magnificent city it is today.

Augustus was plagued by illness throughout his life, yet he lived to be 77 years old—an extreme age at that time. He was a cultured man and wrote many books, although none have survived. The cruelty of his early years is often contrasted with his rather mild nature in later life. He could still resort to cruelty when he felt it necessary, however: he had his own daughter banished because she offended his sense of morality.

Like those of her ancestors, Cleopatra's body was buried in Alexandria, near where the Mosque of the Prophet Daniel now stands, but the actual graves of Cleopatra and Marc Antony have either been destroyed or have not yet been rediscovered. Fascination with the life and times of Cleopatra has persisted, however. Late in the nineteenth century, the government of Egypt donated two obelisks (huge, tapered stone pillars) to Great Britain and the United States. The obelisks are known as Cleopatra's Needles, even though they have no known connection to her. For centuries, they guarded a building in Alexandria, until one of them was toppled by an earthquake. Carved from red granite, they are nearly 70 feet tall. The obelisk in Great Britain now stands on the banks of the Thames River; the one given to the United States stands in New York City's Central Park.

A relic from Cleopatra's time: the red granite obelisk, illustrated in this engraving. One of these obelisks can be found in Great Britain and another in New York City's Central Park. There is no substantive connection between the obelisks and the Egyptian Queen.

In the 1980s, an exploration team led by experienced underwater explorer Franck Goddio began to explore under decades of deposits and several feet of murky water in Alexandria. They were searching for remnants of the ancient city that had slipped under the sea in the fourth century A.D. after a series of severe earthquakes and tidal waves. Most of all, they were looking for the palace of Queen Cleopatra.

In 1996, funded by the Hilti Foundation of Liechtenstein and using historical documents as a guide, Goddio and his team discovered the location of the ancient Royal Quarter of Alexandria. This first mission uncovered statues, ceramics, and columns from this part of the old city. Goddio's team also found the island of Antirhodos, where one of Cleopatra's palaces had been built, and the peninsula where Antony sequestered himself after his defeat at Actium.

Using sophisticated electronic surveys, which provided more data than any other existing tools, the team launched a second mission to the site in 1997. They found two remarkably preserved sphinxes (a stone figure with a lion's body and a human head). To the ancient Egyptians, such statues signified great wisdom. One of the sphinxes is believed to be a representation of Ptolemy XII, Cleopatra's father. Also resurrected from the water were a very rare statue of the Great Priest of Isis, and a large head carved of black granite that is thought to be Augustus. A shipwreck was discovered in the harbor, as well as wooden remains of a pier dating from the fifth century B.C. Goddio also found evidence that Alexander the Great moored his ships at Antirhodos before his city was built. In 1998, Goddio and television's Discovery Channel entered a partnership to produce films on these underwater discoveries. Also in that year, Goddio published a book called *Alexandria: the Submerged Royal Quarters*, based on his explorations of the region.

Will such scientific research one day allow us walk the same streets where Cleopatra and Marc Antony walked? Could we find ourselves in the palace room where she tumbled out of a blanket to confront Caesar? Might we wander the halls where she paced, looking for ways to preserve the honor of her ancestors? No one knows for sure, of course, but perhaps it is explorations like Franck Goddio's, which probe the mysteries of ancient cultures, that will keep alive our fascination with Cleopatra VII, the mysterious queen of the Nile.

CHRONOLOGY

69 B.C.	Cleopatra is born in Alexandria, Egypt
60	Julius Caesar, Marcus Crassus, and Gnaeus Pompey form the First Triumvirate in Rome
59–58	Ptolemy XII goes to Rome to secure Egyptian independence; the following year Cleopatra VII's older sisters seize the throne while their father is away
55	Ptolemy XII retakes the throne of Egypt and executes his daughter Berenice
51	Cleopatra VII and Ptolemy XIII become co-rulers of Egypt upon the death of Ptolemy XII
49–48	Ptolemy XIII's regents force Cleopatra to flee Egypt; she returns to Alexandria to face Ptolemy XIII's army the following year. Pompey is killed; Caesar arrives in Alexandria and meets Cleopatra
47	Ptolemy XIII dies attempting to escape Roman forces; Caesar declares Cleopatra and her youngest brother, Ptolemy XIV, co-rulers of Egypt; Cleopatra's son, Caesarion, is born
46	Cleopatra travels to Rome for Caesar's triumphal march
44	Caesar is assassinated on March 15; Cleopatra returns to Alexandria
43	Ptolemy XIV is poisoned upon Cleopatra's order; the Second Triumvirate is established in Rome
41	Antony invites Cleopatra to Tarsus; Antony returns with Cleopatra to Alexandria; Cleopatra's sister, Arsinoë, is executed
40	Cleopatra gives birth to twins; Antony marries Octavia, Octavian's half-sister
37–36	Cleopatra and Antony are married in Syria; Cleopatra's son, Ptolemy Philadelphus, is born
34	Antony honors Cleopatra with the "donations of Alexandria"
31–30	Cleopatra and Antony are defeated at the Battle of Actium; Octavian takes Alexandria, Antony commits suicide; Cleopatra is taken prisoner and commits suicide; the Ptolemaic dynasty ends

The Reign of the Ptolemies*

323 B.C.	Alexander the Great—conquers Egypt; lays plans for the city of Alexandria
323–285	Ptolemy I Sotor (Greek for "savior")—founds the dynasty and expands his empire through alliances and marriages; establishes the great library of Alexandria
285–246	Ptolemy II Philadelphus, son of Ptolemy I—expands the library of Alexandria and develops a thriving agricultural and commercial society
246–221	Ptolemy III Euergetes, son of Ptolemy II—is victorious in the Third Syrian War
221–205	Ptolemy IV Philopator, son of Ptolemy III—a weak ruler who loses much of the Ptolemaic province of Syria; his reign is marked by numerous uprisings
205–180	Ptolemy V Epiphanes—named king at age five after his father's death and the murder of his mother; marries Cleopatra I and loses most of Egypt's foreign possessions
180–145	Ptolemy VI Philomator, son of Ptolemy V—governs with his mother until her death in 176; he marries his sister, Cleopatra II, and reunites the realm with Roman intervention
145	Ptolemy VII Neos Philopator, son of Ptolemy VI—is deposed and executed by his uncle, Ptolemy VIII Euergetes II
145–116	Ptolemy VIII—marries Ptolemy VII's mother, Cleopatra II; brings civil war and economic collapse to Egypt
116–81	Ptolemy IX Sotor II (also called Lathyrus)—rules with his brother Ptolemy X Alexander I and his mother, Cleopatra III; becomes sole ruler in 88
107–88	Ptolemy X—co-rules with Ptolemy IX; Egypt engages in war with Syria
80	Ptolemy XI Alexander II, son of Ptolemy X—marries Berenice III, the widow of Ptolemy IX; later murders her and is killed in retribution by the citizens of Alexandria
80–51	Ptolemy XII Auletes, son of Ptolemy IX—marries his sister Cleopatra V; gives birth to Cleopatra VII

CHRONOLOGY

51–47	Ptolemy XIII Theos Philopator, son of Ptolemy XII—the brother of Cleopatra VII; dies while attempting to escape Romans after a struggle with Cleopatra for the Egyptian throne
47–44	Ptolemy XIV Theos Philopator II—another son of Ptolemy XII and the youngest brother of Cleopatra VII; he is reportedly poisoned by Cleopatra
40–30	Ptolemy XV Caesar (Caesarion)—presumably the son of Julius Caesar and Cleopatra VII; he reigns with his mother and is murdered by Octavian
51–30	Cleopatra VII—holds successive reigns with Ptolemy XIII, XIV, and XV; the Ptolemaic dynasty ends with her death

*all dates are approximate

Books

Brooks, Polly S. *Cleopatra: Goddess of Egypt, Enemy of Rome.* New York: HarperCollins, 1995.

Crosher, Judith. *Ancient Egypt.* New York: Viking, 1992.

Foreman, Laura. *Cleopatra's Palace: In Search of a Legend.* New York: Discovery Books, 1999.

Foss, Michael. *The Search for Cleopatra.* New York: Arcade Publishing, 1998.

Green, Robert. *Cleopatra.* New York: Franklin Watts, 1996.

Hart, George. *Exploring the Past.* San Diego: Harper, 1992.

Huzar, Eleanor G. *Marc Antony: A Biography.* Minneapolis, Minn.: University of Minnesota Press, 1978.

Jenkins, Ernestine. *A Glorious Past: Ancient Egypt, Ethiopia, and Nubia.* New York: Chelsea House, 1995.

Nardo, Don. *The Importance of Julius Caesar.* San Diego, Calif.: Lucent Books, 1997.

Roberts, Russell. *Rulers of Ancient Egypt.* San Diego, Calif.: Lucent Books, 1999.

Smith, Brenda. *Egypt of the Pharaohs.* San Diego, Calif.: Lucent Books, 1996.

Websites

The British Museum—Ancient Egypt
   http://www.ancientegypt.co.uk

Middle East Online—Article on Cleopatra Exhibit
   http://www.middle-east online.com/English/Features/Apr2001/British %20Museum%20explores%20true%20image%20of%20Cleopatra.htm

Women's History—Cleopatra in Art, Literature, and Film
   http://womenhistory.about.com/cs/cleopatraimages

INDEX

INDEX

Rose Blue is the author of numerous books for children and young adults. Two of her books were adapted for young people's specials aired on NBC television. She is a graduate of Brooklyn College with a master's degree from Bank Street College of Education.

Corinne J. Naden, a graduate of New York University, is a freelance writer and editor. A former journalist in the U.S. Navy and children's book editor in New York City, she has written and co-authored more than 60 books for children and young adults.

Matina S. Horner was president of Radcliffe College and associate professor of psychology and social relations at Harvard University. She is best known for her studies of women's motivation, achievement, and personality development. Dr. Horner has served on several national boards and advisory councils, including those of the National Science Foundation, Time Inc., and the Women's Research and Education Institute. She earned her B.A. from Bryn Mawr College and her Ph.D. from the University of Michigan, and holds honorary degrees from many colleges and universities, including Mount Holyoke, Smith, Tufts, and the University of Pennsylvania.